'Some people appear not to have moods. A friend said when we were discussing the idea of this book: "Moods? I thought those were things that women and teenagers had!"

People increasingly understand how by their own efforts they can keep themselves physically healthy: by sensible eating, not smoking, drinking in moderation and taking regular exercise. The aim of this book is to describe some of the equally simple steps needed to maintain your psychological health. The most important of these is to learn to recognize and accept "bad" moods rather than suppress them.'

Ros Holmes is a counsellor and part-time sheep farmer. Jeremy Holmes is a consultant psychiatrist and psychotherapist, and obstetrician to Ros's sheep. They live in North Devon with their son.

Also available in Orion paperback

THE GOOD MOOD GUIDE

MOOD GUIDE

How to Embrace Your Pain and Face Your Fears

ROS & JEREMY HOLMES

ORION

To Daphne and Erroll Bruce, and Tudor Trevor

An Orion Paperback
First published in Great Britain by J. M. Dent Ltd in 1993.
This paperback edition published in 1994 by Orion Books Ltd,
Orion House, 5 Upper St Martin's Lane, London WC2H 9EA.

Reissued 1998

A CIP catalogue record for this book
is available from the British Library.

ISBN: 0 75282 584 4

Printed and bound in Great Britain by
The Guernsey Press Co. Ltd, Guernsey, C.I.

CONTENTS

ACKNOWLEDGEMENTS

Books don't spring fully formed from the imagination. They contain the accumulated experience and wisdom of many people channelled through the minds of the authors. We would like to thank particularly our parents and children who have had, willy nilly, to endure our moods – good and bad – and have equally exposed us to theirs and set us thinking about learning to live with them in the first place.

We are also greatly indebted to our wider families and the friends, colleagues, teachers, therapists, clients and patients who have all contributed, wittingly and unwittingly, to the making of this book.

Thich Nhat Hanh and Annabel Laity have had an incalculable influence; this book would not have been written had we not encountered their writings and teaching

Victoria Zinovieff, Glenn and Judith Roberts, Anna Hodson and Pat Millner have all made special contributions both through their own ideas, and by helping to modify and fine-tune ours. To them too, our deepest gratitude.

The book is illustrated with many examples. Each of these, we hope, rings true. All were sparked off by experiences which we have encountered in ourselves, our families, friends or patients. But all are fictitious. They represent amalgamations, transformations and modifications of real life, partly in the interests of anonymity, partly to heighten the point they illustrate, partly because that is what our imaginations seem to have chosen to come up with. We hope they are accurate enough to resemble anyone's experience, while being identical to no one's.

PART ONE

The Methods

CHAPTER 1
THE ECOLOGY OF MOODS

'... suffer a sea-change

Into something rich and strange.' (*The Tempest*)

If, on meeting, a friend asks 'How are you ?', your most likely reply will be 'Fine', 'O.K.', or 'Very well, thanks'. And, surprisingly, that will probably be the truth. Most of us do feel all right most of the time. And yet there is an enormous amount of suffering in the world. Even in our relatively secure and comfortable Western society one in five of us will have experienced a major

> *one in five of us will have experienced a major loss or setback in the previous year*

loss or setback in the previous year: a bereavement, the loss of a job, a serious illness affecting ourselves or someone close to us, major financial difficulties, trouble with the police. If we look back over five years, more than half of us will have suffered adversity or loss. But somehow we cope. Just as our bodies have defence mechanisms for dealing with infection which keep us reasonably healthy, so the mind has ways of dealing with loss and stress which enable us to remain psychologically balanced and more or less cheerful.

But that is not the whole story. There is often a price to pay for being able to cope. By putting painful thoughts and feelings to one side we manage to keep going, but at the expense of inner feelings of deadness or physical symptoms. We may become emotionally blocked, or victims of chronically suppressed anger and anxiety. A great amount of distress does surface as family discord, in alcohol and drug abuse, in chronic discontent and unhappiness. In the US 75 million people (out of a total of 250 million) visit their doctors every year needing help with emotional disorders. In phlegmatic Britain 3 million of us visit our GP each year, and one third of these visits are related to psychological difficulties. The suffering that goes with loss lies at the root of much emotional distress. Among those with clinical depression, the proportion who have experienced an unhappy loss or painful emotional event in the previous year goes up from one fifth to two thirds.

EXAMPLE: UNEMPLOYMENT AND DEPRESSION

Jason, a normally cheerful and friendly young man in his early twenties, lost his job as a plasterer when, due to economic recession, the building firm which he worked for began laying off workers. He started to feel miserable and jumpy, useless and bored. After a few months of unemployment he was taken on by another firm, this time as a self-employed sub-contractor. But now his anxiety increased as he imagined that the work he was doing was not up to scratch, and that he would be found out and sacked at any moment. There seemed no way out, and one evening he went to a nearby bridge and thought seriously about throwing himself off. He suddenly realized what he was doing and this seemed to jolt him into thinking about himself and his story. He had always felt overshadowed by his academically successful older brother, and never felt good enough for his ambitious father who was keen for both his sons to 'do well'. Slow at school, he could never remember the date of his birthday and the girl he sat next to always had to remind him when it was. He found reading and writing difficult and he was put into the 'remedial' class when he entered secondary school. There he was well liked and became the joker of the class, but he resented being seen as different and 'stupid'. He left school with no qualifications, but got an apprenticeship in the building trade and soon began to enjoy his work and found that he was good at it. His self-esteem improved, he found a steady girlfriend, and life felt good – until he lost his job. As he thought about these things he was overcome with a wave of anger towards everyone who he felt had underestimated and undervalued him: his father, the school, his employer, 'the government'. At first he was confused and guilty about his angry feelings; he decided to confront his father, and, to his surprise found him much more receptive than he had anticipated – he told Jason about his own periods of depression. Jason's suicidal feelings did not return and he gradually began to feel better. Soon afterwards he left home and set up with his girlfriend.

TRANSFORMATION VERSUS SUPPRESSION

There are many ways of dealing with the mental pain that accompanies the difficulties and disappointments that life presents us with. We can hope the passage of time will lessen the intensity of our miserable feelings. Perhaps we summon up the courage to talk to a friend or family member about what is bothering or hurting us. We may scream at someone if they will let us, which sometimes makes us feel better. We may try to suppress the problem by trying not to think about it, or by blotting it out with drink or drugs. We may retreat into illness.

EXAMPLE: SWALLOWING ANGER

Caroline, a single parent in her twenties, had brought up her daughter on her own very successfully. Then she met another man whom she liked, and became pregnant by him. After the baby was born he was attentive and loving and she hoped that here at last was a man with whom she could share the burdens and pleasures of parenthood. But it was not to be. He drifted off leaving her once more on her own, this time with two children including a very demanding baby. She continued to look after the children as best she could, but began to feel increasingly run down and developed persistent tonsillitis for which she was prescribed several courses of antibiotics. Finally, with her temperature in the 100s and barely able to speak or swallow for the pain in her throat, she called for her mother to come and help. All went well for a day or two, but suddenly a furious row broke out between mother and daughter in which Caroline screamed and screamed and hurled abuse at her mother accusing her of being moralizing and neglectful and interfering all at the same time! As the row subsided Caroline suddenly discovered that she felt better, and above all her throat felt clear and she could talk normally again.

At last the anger and disappointment she had felt towards the baby's father had come out. Her mother's acceptance of it (not unqualified – she got a few jibes in too) allowed her 'bad' feelings to be expressed, the loss of her hopes to begin to be mourned.

When we are physically injured, the body will repair itself in an orderly and highly

> *When we are physically injured, the body will repair itself*

> *We have within us a similar set of psychological responses to help us cope with and overcome mental pain and loss*

efficient way. Blood vessels contract to prevent bleeding; infection is warded off by the immune system; new skin grows to cover the breach; finally a scar forms to give the affected area strength and endurance. We have within us a similar set of psychological responses to help us cope with and overcome mental pain and loss. Caroline's anger and tears and reconciliation were all part of the mourning response – a healthy way of dealing with her unhappiness, which enabled her, once her feelings were released, to continue with her life. Through expressing feelings in this way, often in the safety of a close relationship, we get them into perspective, so that an open emotional wound becomes a bearable scar. But many of us, through our upbringing and circumstances, find this very difficult. We block off our feelings, don't want to 'burden' others with them, feel humiliated by our 'weakness'. We try to escape from pain by locking it away and putting on a brave face or by collapsing into helplessness.

PSYCHOLOGICAL SELF-HELP

People increasingly understand how by their own efforts they can keep themselves physically healthy: by sensible eating, not smoking, drinking in moderation and taking regular exercise. The aim of this book is to describe some of the equally simple steps needed to maintain your psychological health. The most important of these is to learn to recognize and accept 'bad' moods rather than suppress them. If your marriage is making you unhappy, or someone you love has died or left you and you are missing them 'badly', it is surely 'good' to feel 'bad'? So, although we call this the 'good mood guide' it could equally

have been called the 'good guide to bad moods' (except that doesn't trip off the tongue so easily). It is based on the recognition that suffering is an intrinsic part of life – just as day goes with night, beauty with ugliness, love with hate – and on the possibility of using this insight to find the 'good' aspects of 'bad' moods.

The way we all feel is strongly influenced by our perception of things. Although circumstances set the scene for bad moods it is because we expect things to go right, losses never to occur, that we are so devastated when they do. If, as children, we had the experience of a loving family in which our rage and disappointment and envy was balanced by love and security and an acceptance of our 'bad' feelings, then, as adults, when things go 'wrong' we have a bank of memories which tell us, without our being aware of it, that to be miserable is not wrong, and that things will come 'right' in the end.

It is only too easy to attribute our bad feelings to whatever is causing them and so see them as inevitable and unalterable. But our mood – depression or hate or fear – is our reaction to what has happened to us, and therefore open to change.

When we feel bad our first thought may be to get rid of the bad feelings, to jettison them if we possibly can. But we also know how hard that can be. Moods sit on us like heavy weights. Even if we do manage to put them down for a while they may creep back, like a monster in a horror movie. This book is not about abandoning bad moods, but about transforming them,

transform your stumbling blocks into stepping stones

finding a positive aspect to them, so that a heavy burden becomes light. We shall show you how to get your bad moods to work for you rather than against you – to make them move so that they change into useful companions. In this book you will find ways to transform your stumbling blocks into stepping stones.

MOOD ECOLOGY

This approach could be called 'ecological'. The term ecology comes from the Greek word *oikos* meaning a house – the study of organisms in relation to the environment which houses them. The self can be thought of as a house – 'a house with many mansions'. That self houses all the different feelings, hopes and desires that you possess, and which sometimes possess you. Some are 'good' – love, tenderness, generosity, concern. Others are 'bad' – hate, greed, apathy, selfishness, despair. We put 'good' and 'bad' in inverted commas because from the ecological perspective there is no good or bad – you are just one complete being. We tend to split ourselves into the good bits and the bad bits. For example, we may like our bright eyes and strong hands, but find our knobbly knees, flabby tummy or thinning hair difficult to accept, just as people tend to favour some parts of their country over others – some love the open skies of the flatlands but hate narrow lanes and deep dells, whereas others dislike dull plains but adore secret valleys and dramatic beaches. But the world, like our bodies, is a whole – one interconnected set of places and spaces. From the ecological perspective the same is true of our moods. If we try to 'cut them out', they return to mock and torment us. We can no more eliminate bad moods altogether than we can cut off the left-hand end of a stick by dividing it into two. We need to accept all our moods for what they are – including the bad ones – valuing them as parts of our totality.

EXAMPLE: A GRIEF DENIED

Margaret was a conscientious hard-working doctor whose husband had died tragically – he drank too much and had inhaled his vomit after an alcoholic evening – when she was thirty, leaving her with two small daughters. She immediately returned to her parents who brought up the girls while she went out to work. Everyone was impressed by her efficiency and correctness. She rebuffed any suitors, saying there was no room in her life for romance – she had her patients and her daughters to think of. The years went by, her daughters left home, her parents died and she was left on her own. Every year, around the time of her husband's death, she would feel a little 'low', but one year the feeling persisted. She became more and more miserable and worried. She berated herself for her 'weakness', for the fact that she was not doing her work properly and neglecting her usually immaculate appearance and previously tidy house. To her, depression was anathema, grief 'unnecessary', anger an indulgence – and yet she felt all these things. Unable to accept her 'bad' self, she fell into a spiral of depression in which the more miserable she became the more wicked she appeared in her own eyes. Only when she started to see that her feeling of loss and emptiness, her anger at her dead husband, her child-like emotions of helplessness and fear were legitimate, did she begin to recover.

If you think your hunger is 'bad', you may deny your need for food, starve, become unbearably hungry and secretly stuff yourself with the very treats you are trying to avoid. You have split yourself into a public 'good' bit, and a secret 'bad' part, rather than seeing your hunger and greed and craving as parts of yourself which need to be recognized and accepted as symptoms of a deeper need. 'Bad' moods and impulses should be made friends with, understood, cherished – though not necessarily indulged. If the 'badness' remains underground it is a subversive element which you cannot control. Approaching the diet problem ecologically would mean committing yourself to optimally healthy eating. As you begin to think about the effects on your body of every-

Anger expressed to the right person in the right way can lead to reconciliation

thing you eat, you will begin to desire the things that you believe will enhance your health. The satisfaction this brings penetrates far deeper than the sensations in your mouth.

An 'ecological' approach to mood transformation empha-sizes the interconnectedness of things, and takes account of the cyclical nature of our being and of our relationship to the environment. Many 'bad' things can become useful to us if we learn to recycle them properly. Through composting, manure becomes fertilizer which in turn can feed a beautiful rose bush. Recycled waste can be used to used to heat houses. Out of chaos comes structure; breaking down the old provides the building blocks for the new. Similarly, out of depression can come a sense of a loss mourned and a new beginning. Anger expressed to the right person in the right way can lead to reconciliation. Anxiety spurs us to action to try new things.

An ecological approach does not mean that all ills can be peacefully overcome. There are harmful substances like DDT –

usually man-made – that cannot be transformed and do need more drastic remedies if they are to be rendered harmless. So too the mind can be poisoned by hatred or mistrust. Poisons can often be eliminated from the body by neutral substances that are unaffected by them, and similarly we may need the support of family and friends – and sometimes professional help – to help us detoxify some of our most negative emotions.

CHANGE: QUICK AND SLOW

Although the ecological perspective emphasizes how we are embedded in a complex web of relationships, this does not mean that change has to be difficult. Changing one small thing in your life can be the start of an overall rethinking of your priorities.

EXAMPLE: SAVED BY DIRT

Grace decided finally that life was not worth living and, placing her head in the gas oven (this was in the days before 'safe' gas), lay down to die. While waiting for the drowsiness to come over her she noticed that her hair was sticking to sides of the stove: 'This oven is absolutely filthy,' she thought to herself and, turning the gas off, proceeded to clean it furiously. By the time she had finished her suicidal feelings had gone.

Transformation is not usually a matter of blinding insight, but rather of slow, steady effort applied daily over weeks, months and years. We need to integrate new ways of being into our routines until they become habits. From an early age you have probably found methods of dealing with pain and unhappiness: having a hot bath or going to bed with a hot water bottle, to take two fairly innocuous examples. The aim is not to stop these tried and tested methods, but to use them, so they become not means of escape but ways of giving you the opportunity to recognize, touch and accept your pain. In the comfort of your bath you can brood on yourself and your feelings. Even more problematic remedies like getting drunk, or binge eating can be a spur to change when we reach 'rock bottom' and realize we just cannot go on in the old way.

This book does not offer a crash course. The habits of a lifetime cannot and should not be altered overnight. The old donkey remains cowed by his burden long after it has been removed. But we need to start somewhere. The aim is simple: to live more contentedly and harmoniously. We need to awaken our awareness of breathing, sitting, walking, eating, smiling – being. There is no other way to set out on a journey than by putting one foot in front of the other. If we can learn to live in the present, to accept reality as it is, we can leave the future to take care of itself.

Exercise: Breathing brings you back to yourself

You can start now. Set this book aside for a moment and, sitting comfortably, breathe in slowly and deeply to a count of four or five. Then let the breath flow out naturally. Feel your abdomen rise and fall gently as the air enters and leaves your body. As you do so, focus your attention on the breath as it passes in and out of your nostrils. This simple action is a first step in bringing you back to yourself, calming yourself, making you feel more complete and whole and in control of your life.

EMPOWERMENT AND 'MOOD-BROODING'

This book is based on the principles of ecological aware-ness, empowerment and 'entering' your mood. We have

> *you have a vast store of untapped creativity and healing power within you*

already mentioned ecological awareness and must now briefly introduce the second and third of these. Empowerment is based on the idea that if people were better able to handle their own moods, their need for medical help and recourse to tranquillizers and antidepressants would be less. It also contains the idea that you have a vast store of untapped creativity and healing power within you, if only you can find ways to reach it. That is another reason why getting rid of 'bad' moods is not a good idea. They are part of you and the energy within them needs to be harnessed to healthy rather than destructive ends. The force of your anger can be used for self-assertion, the depth of your sadness can demonstrate the profundity of your feelings. There is much within you of which your conscious self is unaware. You need to find ways to tap into these silent areas of the self.

To change something you have first to understand it from the inside. We call this 'entering' your mood, or 'mood-brood-ing'. If you can look under the bonnet of yourself, when some-thing goes wrong you will be able to fix it, or to ask for expert help in an informed way. You need to be able to recognize, name, meet and explore your moods. Once you have entered your mood you will learn not to be afraid of it, to 'touch' the mood in an 'inner dialogue' in which you greet it as an old friend: 'Hello anger, what are you trying to say to me ?' As well as entering your mood with your mind and finding ways to describe and express it, you need also to pay attention to your body. Your state of mind has a profound affect on the way you look, face the world and hold yourself physically.

This process of entering a mood is the first step toward its transformation. Self-observation is in itself transformative, in an extraordinary way. You start to reflect, rather than act, on your own feelings.

EXAMPLE: ACADEMIC HACKLES

John, a lecturer, began to feel bored and irritated when a senior member of his profession came to give a day-long seminar at work. As the lecture droned on he found himself thinking that he would slip away, go home and do some gardening. His feelings of restlessness and boredom continued and he found himself making a rather aggressive point in the discussion. He began to feel in a thoroughly 'bad' mood. Then he remembered the breathing technique mentioned earlier. Taking a few breaths he was brought back to himself. He decided to 'enter' his mood. As he did so he saw how he felt threatened by this senior male who had come muscling into his territory. Just at that moment the lecturer was talking about dogs snarling at each other in mock-fighting! John suddenly saw the absurdity of his rivalry. 'Entering' his boredom and irritation in this way released the block which made him feel threatened and from then on he was able to enjoy and participate in the seminar.

Exercise: Transforming your mood

You may like to try something similar. There are three simple steps. The first is to set the book aside once more and repeat the breathing exercise we suggested just now. Second, once you are breathing calmly, think about the last time you were in a 'bad' mood. Try to picture the mood. Perhaps an image will suggest itself. (Churchill called his depression 'the black dog'.) Perhaps you see yourself doing what you would really like to: letting rip at the customers at work, telling your boss what you think of him. Perhaps you see yourself curled up in a foetal position, longing to be soothed and held. Perhaps something is 'on your back', pressing you down, which you long to shake off. The third step is the transformation of the mood. Allow the image gradually to change as you watch it with your inner eye. Don't decide in advance what will happen, just let it emerge.

EXAMPLE: THE RUNAWAY HORSE

Liz had a dream in which she was riding bareback on a dark stallion careering through a dense forest. She felt terrified and helpless, convinced she would fall off and be injured. Gradually she gained control over the horse until eventually she cantered out of the woods, uplifted with a feeling of exhilaration and mastery.

Whatever image comes into your mind – and it is not always as easy or dramatic as this illustration – comes from within you and needs to be cherished as part of the creative power which you can harness and start to use to bring your 'bad' moods under control, like the rider in the dream. Three steps are needed: control – hold – let go. We shall encourage you to practise these many times throughout this book. Breathing is the means of control, bringing your feelings back to yourself. You then hold your feelings in your imagination as you continue to breathe. Finally, as you detach yourself from your feelings, you will see them transform before your inner eye – a sea-change into something rich and strange.

Exercise: Recording 'bad' habits

When moods are persistent it can be helpful to 'enter' them more systematically using pencil and paper. This can also have surprisingly powerful results. As an experiment take some minor habit or feeling which bothers you: let us say your tendency to nibble when you are not really hungry, to have a drink routinely after coming home from work or to shout unnecessarily at your children. Without trying to alter anything, simply record the number of times you carry out the unwelcome action. You will be amazed by the effect of this simple method of awareness. You will notice that the frequency of your 'bad' habit invariably reduces if you watch yourself doing it!

We hope you will find your own 'answers' to your moods, choosing what suits you best out of the range of useful techniques that are available. We shall follow the ecological principle of not trying to eliminate bad moods but to find ways in which you can accept and live with them and release the energy and creativity which is often locked up in them.

HEDGEHOG AND FOX

The Oxford philosopher Isaiah Berlin once divided thinkers into two main types which he called 'hedgehogs' and 'foxes'. Hedgehogs have one big idea, and once they have got it they tend to curl up in a ball and hold onto it; foxes rush around sniffing at lots of different things and are excited by all of

> *the way to overcome bad moods is not to try to get rid of them but to accept and transform them*

them. This book has one hedgehog in it: that the way to overcome bad moods is not to try to get rid of them but to accept and transform them – beating swords of anger into ploughshares of self-assertion, turning the stuckness of depression into the healing tears of grief.

The rest is pure fox – we offer many different methods for overcoming moods, all of which, if they can be integrated into your daily life, can lead to a permanent improvement in wellbeing. Both approaches are needed. To reach the treasure the hero of the fairy story needs his seven-league boots and also the help of many magical creatures. You will need an alliance between the parental 'seven-league' part of yourself and the child-like magic part if you are, as in a fairy story, to transform 'bad' into 'good'.

SUMMARY

- Depression, fear, anger and envy belong to us as much as their counterparts lightheartedness, courage, love and fulfilment.
- The present moment is the point at which we have control – the past has gone, the future is not yet here.
- You are the absolute expert on yourself. Develop your powers of self-observation.
- Aim for transformation, integration, wholeness. If you dislike and try to eliminate aspects of yourself you will be depleted. You may have to release blocks in order to discover your true feelings.
- Control – contain – let go: breathe – visualize – transform: these are the basic methods by which 'bad' moods can turn into 'good'.

CHAPTER 2
WHAT ARE MOODS FOR ?

'There is a great deal of unmapped country within us which would have to be taken into account in an explanation of our gusts and storms.' (George Eliot)

Most people have a very simple aim in life: to be happy. And yet happiness seems so elusive. If only, we dream… If only I had that job, house, lover, money, holiday, then I really would be happy. But we all know in our hearts that it's not that easy. Money can't buy you love – although circumstances profoundly affect our moods: a beautiful day, a phone call from a friend, getting a good job, a pay rise, a smile from our lover can all make a huge difference. What matters is the effect circumstances have on our inner world, the way they make us feel good about ourselves. If we can assimilate good experiences and make use of them then the effects will endure, but if we lack receptiveness bad moods will continue to dominate. We are hungry for happiness, but if our throats are too narrow we are unable to be nourished by good experiences.

With moods as with many other things, rather unfairly, nothing succeeds like success. If you are in a good mood, then good things 'happen' to you, the phone does ring, your lover does smile; if not, then not.

EXAMPLE: THE WISE MAN AND THE TRAVELLERS

This is rather like the story of the wise man sitting at the roadside who was asked by a traveller arriving in his village,

'What sort of people live in this neighbourhood, brother?' The man turned the question back, 'What sort of people lived in the last village?' 'Oh, villains and ruffians the lot of them,' came the reply. 'Well I expect you'll find the people round here much the same,' responded the man. When a second traveller arrived asking the same question, the wise man answered as before. This time the traveller said that the people he had come from had been kind and hospitable. 'Oh well,' concluded the sage, 'you'll probably find people round here pretty friendly and helpful too.'

Beauty is in the eye of the beholder. The way we see the world is an expression of our moods and influences the kinds of experiences we have.

> *The way we see the world is an expression of our moods and influences the kinds of experiences we have*

Happiness, or otherwise, comes from within. There is much we cannot control in our lives: the accident of when and where and to whom we were born, our genetic makeup, our parents, the society in which we live. But we can control our reactions to these circumstances. We can nourish our better self, tend our positive attributes. What we make of what we are is up to us. The pessimist's cup is always half empty and falling; the optimist's half full and rising.

For most of us our moods, our inner world, seem as hard to control as external circumstances. Children, who tend to take things literally, are sometimes surprised to be told they have 'got out of bed on the wrong side', especially when their beds are firmly pressed against the wall and there appears to be only one way to get out of them. But bad moods are rather like that impenetrable wall. They tower over you and force you to do their bidding. It often seems as difficult to get away from feelings of despair or loneliness or envy or fury as it would have been to break down the wall and get out of bed on the 'right' side. Telling yourself to snap out of it rarely seems to work, much less being told to by someone else. But, as we shall see later, miracles can happen. There are ways through the wall of your feelings. You can, through transformation, go through the looking glass or the wardrobe, find the other end of the rainbow.

DEALING WITH BAD MOODS: AVOIDANCE AND DISTRACTION

There are many ways of coping with bad moods, and it is important to be aware of what they are.

Blame
The first thing that many people do when they feel bad is to blame someone or something for it. 'Of course I am in a bad mood – I've had lousy day with the kids, there's no money to pay the bills, and you come home late and full of beer.' 'It's all your fault I'm home late. I've had a terrible time with the boss. I knew it would be nothing but nagging when I got in. Do you blame me for dropping in at the pub? At least I get some sympathy there' – and so on.

Avoidance
A second favourite method is avoidance. We are all adept at putting bad things to the back of our minds, hoping they will go away or solve themselves. We treat our problems like a room that needs tidying which we avoid going into.

Distraction
Another classic method is to distract ourselves from misery and discomfort by seeking pleasure or oblivion. The

anaesthetic effects of drink or drugs are perhaps the commonest means. The excitement of sex is another – an affair or flirtation is often a temporary escape from despair. You may resort to comfort eating: without consciously being aware of feeling lonely, suddenly you find yourself, in defiance of your diet, ravenously indulging in sweet things.

Rationalization

A fourth common method of dealing with bad moods is to rationalize them. A tearful baby in want of security and stimulation is deemed to be hungry or teething, or not quite well. Adults blame their moods on the stars, the weather, 'the time of the month', the menopause or a 'virus'.

Denial

Sometimes bad moods may simply be denied. They are clearly perceptible to those around us, in our voice and our gestures, but we are

> *Sometimes bad moods may simply be denied*

trapped in a habitual pattern, unwilling to recognize how we feel. How many of us have not, when asked 'Is something the matter?', self-betrayingly replied between clenched teeth 'No, nothing, nothing at all'?

These methods of suppressing bad moods have their uses, indeed we all resort to them at times. But they can end up perpetuating the bad moods rather than helping us to integrate them. Blaming others leads to retaliation and escalating rows which may leave you and your partner feeling even worse off than before. What started as a distraction and a comfort – alcohol or drugs – may end up as an addiction, possibly more destructive than the mood it originally was designed to overcome. Tucking away something unpleasant often means that it returns in an exaggerated form later. The unpaid bill you tried to forget about becomes a final demand, with interest. If you feel angry with someone but ignore it, you may end up feeling angry with everyone and anything, including, most importantly of all, yourself, and suffering the blank cut-offness of depression.

We shall explore ways of dealing with bad moods other than by these common coping methods. We need to find the meaning behind our moods, discover a message in them which, if listened to, can be positive. This is not possible if they are swept under the carpet. We shall encourage you to get to know your bad moods, observe them, stay with them, befriend them, touch them, hold them like a crying child: 'Hello sadness, let me comfort you'. We shall suggest ways to express your emotional states that can release you from the burden of suppressed 'bad' feelings. But first, why do we have moods at all, what are they for ?

WHY DO WE HAVE BAD MOODS ?

Pain is a signal that tells us there is something wrong

As children we may have wondered why we feel pain: why should nettles sting, fires burn, pins prick? The most obvious answer is that, given the fragility of living organisms, feeling pain helps us to survive, just as it helped our evolutionary ancestors in the past. Leprosy sufferers, whose illness has deadened pain sensations in their hands and feet, would gladly exchange their scarred and stiffened extremities for the occasional unpleasantness of pain. Pain is a signal that tells us there is something wrong, something that needs to be avoided or changed in the environment. Although moods are more complex than painful sensations, it is helpful to think of bad moods as forms of mental pain. The mood contains an important message for us. But what is that message about ?

MOODS AND MOTHERS (AND FATHERS)

To answer that we need to go back to the beginnings of our lives. A psychoanalyst once said that 'there is no such thing as a baby'. By that he meant there could never be a baby alone, since it would inevitably die, only a baby-and-mother partnership – even Romulus and Remus had a mother-wolf to suckle them. We are from the start related to one another, and our feelings are intimately bound up with our relationships. When his parent, usually but not necessarily his mother, is there, holding him, tuning into him, feeding him, the baby feels good. When she is away, or unresponsive, or preoccupied, he feels bad. His moods depend on the state of this relationship. Through his love for her he learns the positive emotions of excitement, satiation, contentment, joy and happiness. If he becomes separated from his mother he will protest and cry until she returns. If she is delayed, despair will dominate for a while. We can imagine the hope, fear, rage and misery he may be feeling during the separation. On her return she will understand his feelings, soothe and regulate them, and, by naming them, begin to make sense for him of the complex and chaotic medley of moods he is filled with.

Later, as he or she gets older, the child becomes aware of his father, his brothers and sisters, the parents as a couple, and a whole new set of complex emotions are aroused: envy, jealousy, feelings of exclusion and more subtle feelings like boredom and apathy. These bad feelings will be balanced by good moods based on play, companionship and sharing.

Like pain, bad moods are signals, not about the physical world, but about the world of our relationships. A mood is not just a thing in itself to be endured or ignored, it is about someone or something that is important to us. Moods are messages, both to ourselves and to others, which we

> *Moods are messages, both to ourselves and to others, which we need to attend to and learn to 'read'*

need to attend to and learn to 'read'. They have been built into us by our evolutionary history. Early humans lived in groups and needed to function smoothly as a unit for foraging and mutual protection. Groups containing people who could 'read' their own and others' emotional states would have been more successful, so more likely to survive, than those who could not.

As the baby grows, so his dependence on his mother and family lessens, although most of us continue to live in families and groups, and to be intimately attached to a small number of other people – partners, children, parents, friends, workmates – throughout our lives. *The pattern of the early relationship to the mother, where the child signals a mood and the mother responds, starts to be repeated inside the individual*. In this internalized relationship we become parents to ourselves, and, like all parents, vary in the extent to which we respond to our feelings, moods and wishes. There may be a 'bad internal parent' who neglects or attacks us, and this part of ourselves is bound up with the self-sabotage and self-destructiveness that is often a feature of 'bad' moods. There will also be a 'good internal parent' whom we need to cultivate, so becoming more self-attuned and self-responsive. With the assistance of a secure internal parent we can withstand the inevitable failures and misunderstandings of relationships without being plunged into confusion and unhappiness. In this way we can cope with the buffetings of misfortune and the complexity of our ever-changing emotions.

SUMMARY SO FAR :

- Moods help us to survive.
- Moods are signals – we need to learn to listen to them.
- Good parents respect their children's moods. We need to learn to become good parents to ourselves.

CHAPTER 3
WHAT ARE MOODS MADE OF ?

'Show some emotion…' (J. Armatrading)

> A *'mood'* is made up of three parts: physical, emotional and verbal

A 'mood' is made up of three parts: physical, emotional and verbal. We usually associate a mood with a physical sensation. We have butterflies in the stomach when we are afraid, a heavy feeling when depressed, weepiness when sad, tension and clenching of the muscles when angry and floppiness when apathetic. When we are happy we feel as if we are walking on air, skipping through the clover, our hearts bursting with joy. Particularly important are the physical manifestations in the face, for it is there that our moods are reflected. We can tell whether someone is afraid, happy, angry or sad from the look on their face, and by the way they hold their body.

The word e-motion captures the movement of moods – the swirl of feelings and images and memories that are triggered off by (and themselves create) the physical sensations. These are usually described by analogy and metaphor. The purpose of poetry, art and music is to capture emotion through the use of imagery. We are stranded in deserts of boredom, founder in oceans of despair or explode with volcanic eruptions of anger. So linked up are the physical sensations and these images that our bodies may express them: we may be bent double with guilt, twisted with bitterness, flattened by feelings of failure. Our tone of voice is also revealing: it may become harsh, flat, whiny, brittle, or phoney and artificial. We carry within us a history of moods and experiences from the past. If expressions of anger have been sharply punished as children, when the sensations associated with anger arise in us now we are likely to be frightened of them and take immediate avoiding action by suppressing them.

These first two stages of mood formation – the physical and the emotional – go on automatically. We may not be aware of them at all. All we know is that we are in a mood – 'got the hump', 'down in the dumps', 'mad at him', 'shit-scared' – we put a name or a phrase to the mood, and that's it. This is the third 'part' of the mood: the naming of it by the self that experiences it. This depends on a conscious part of the self that can, with effort, detach itself from the mood. The 'I' that is depressed is not completely identified with that depression, but an observer who, integrating the physical sensations and the imagery, concludes 'I am totally depressed'. Totally? A moment's reflection will reveal parts of the self that are not being considered: 'I got up this morning, made some breakfast, opened my letters, cleaned the house, got the children off to school – there are parts of me that are not immobilized by depression'. That may be a start, a small start admittedly, on the long haul out of depression. It is based on the recognition that the self is a complex mixture of many ingredients – positive and negative – and that in a 'mood' one part dominates and

> *A depressed person is like the owner of a stately home who keeps most of his or her property locked up*

blinds us to the good things that are also present. 'The self is a house with many mansions.' A depressed person is like the owner of a stately home who keeps most of his or her property locked up and spends the time miserably huddled in front of a one-bar electric fire with the curtains shut, afraid to stretch, expand, throw open the blinds, light the boiler and enjoy the riches all around.

It is the mood that keeps the self captive in this way, pinned down in one place. To fight against the mood is a struggle, especially as the 'I', although in theory the 'owner' of the house that is the self, often feels powerless. This 'I' is rather like a constitutional monarch who is nominally head of state but is in fact ruled by parliament. We shall show how your 'I' can gain some measure of cooperation with the unruly gang of republican moods that sometimes undermine your power to control your life. We are not suggesting that you meet violence with violence however. Merely locking all the bad moods up will not work. Eventually they will escape again, and renew their attack with even more ferocity. Our solution requires a democratic compromise, a meeting with the moods, seeing their point of view, listening to what they have to say, understanding them and responding to them like a wise leader. In this way the moods can be encouraged to work for rather than against you.

MOODS AND THE SEXES

Some people appear not to have moods. A friend said when we were discussing the idea of this book: 'Moods? I thought those were things that women and teenagers had!'. He was, inevitably, male, and in our unequal and sexist society men are notoriously less good at identifying their moods than women, although no less prone to bad ones. She is expected to know what mood he is in by the way he slams the door when he comes in from work, how he crackles the newspaper or dives for the drinks cupboard. Women have had it drummed into them that it is their job to recognize and smooth out men's moods, and are expected to get on with dealing with their own moods by themselves.

We need to take responsibility for our own lives, including moods, if only because we can, in the end, only change ourselves, not our partners or children. But if we do manage to change we often find that it affects the way people close to us are too. We discussed earlier how the parent – usually but not necessarily the mother – holds and soothes her baby's moods, until he or she is old enough to have developed an 'internal parent' who can do the job unaided. One aim of this book is to help with this process of internal parenting. Men are all too adept at finding women who will 'cope' with them – a continuation of their relationship with their mothers. They could learn to be more tender towards themselves. Women are often expert in looking after their children's and menfolk's moods, but feel guilty about making time and space to look after themselves.

WHY NOW ?

Our differing moods are an essential monitor and regulator of the state of our relationships. Most of the time we just rub along with them – the relationships and the moods – without feeling the need for change. It is usually at moments of heightened emotion that we become motivated enough to want to alter things. It may take a death, the diagnosis of a life-threatening disease, a job loss or a divorce to make our state of mind intolerable and oppressive. In this state of crisis there is great opportunity for deep and beneficial change. We can no longer function or live fully without altering our perceptions, working out our own solutions, opening up new possibilities and trying to find sources of equanimity. The map we have lived by no longer applies. We have to explore new territory, constructing new routes and rules for ourselves. Our defences against pain and misfortune have been breached. We stand naked and alone, but there are countless opportunities for help and guidance if only we can perceive and grasp them. When crises touch our lives we may experience pure unprocessed emotions which are as powerful as falling in love, but here it is pain not joy that goes to the centre of our being – we feel we are drowning in grief, or clinging by our fingers to a precipice of fear.

THE IMPORTANCE OF MOURNING

What we do with these feelings is what makes the difference between being imprisoned or liberated by our moods. Despair may linger as a dull cloud hanging around us. But if we can find a way to penetrate this gloom, putting our unhappiness into words or music or images, or identifying with nature and the seasons, we will see that what we call 'bad' is part of the cycle of life which inevitably leads on to rebirth.

Many mood difficulties can be traced to the way we deal with loss. Grief makes us numb, despairing, angry, restless, apathetic, listless, depressed. Mourning is painful, but if we can endure these feelings and let the process run its course we carry within us a memory of what is lost that strengthens rather than diminishes us. If we cannot let go and so inhibit the mourning response we are disabled.

EXAMPLE: DECISIONS, DECISIONS

Luke, a young man in his late twenties, had enormous difficulty in making his mind up about anything, large or small. Should he trade in his car for a newer one? Marry his long-standing girlfriend? Stay with his job as a teacher, which he did not enjoy but which offered security, or become a freelance musician, which was what he really wanted to do? Buy this shirt or that one? Each question sent him into an agony of indecision. Before a decision had to be made he was in a torment of anxiety; afterwards he was plagued with regrets about the roads not taken. Not surprisingly, his indecisiveness often made those involved with him exasperated and angry.

His parents had divorced when he was young and he had shuttled uncomfortably between them for most of his childhood. Then his father died suddenly of a heart attack. Luke, who was his only child, made the funeral arrangements, and felt, as well as great sadness, a strange sense of relief: his father was finally not there, rather than being tantalizingly just out of reach as he had been for much of his childhood. He also felt a surge of rage – at the fact that his father had been taken from him, at his father for dying when he still felt he needed him, at himself for the worry he had caused him. But this anger was helpful. He suddenly saw how as a child he had never really had an opportunity to protest about the separation of his parents, or mourn the loss of the happy family he would have liked to have had. As an adult he continued this process, by habitually aborting and perpetuating his angry feelings by indecisiveness, and making those around him feel the anger that rightfully belonged to him. He saw too how he placed himself for most of the time in a position of half-completed grief – neither letting go of the old, nor grasping firmly to the new. He began to see how in his indecision he lacked the courage to bear the pain of letting go, and was unable to trust that through mourning he would hold on to what was good, and so enjoy the excitement and promise of new hopes and possibilities.

Each of our lives is like a personal fairy story in which we are faced with a series of obstacles, some apparently insurmountable, but in which we also come across an astonishing number of magical helpers who appear when we are *in extremis*. The

> **The terrors of the imagination are almost always worse than the reality**

witch is just about to catch and devour us, when we throw down an enchanted comb and she becomes tangled in an impenetrable forest. We are in a dark place, the belly of the whale, when we are suddenly thrown safely onto a sunlit beach. We can awaken from our nightmares. The terrors of the imagination are almost always worse than the reality.

Even those who are fortunate enough to have avoided major disappointments, bereavements or tragedies will have times of crisis and turning points in their lives when emotions run strong. Adolescence, marriage, childbirth, children leaving home, promotion, even moving house – all these can stir up feelings which may seem overwhelming at times. It is at these times of disequilibrium that we feel most helpless, often searching desperately for some way to regain balance.

TRANSFORMING MOODS

Overcoming Fear

We have described the three ingredients which make up a mood: physical sensations and bodily changes, a set of memories and images, the name which the self puts on them. Just as the mechanic will strip down an engine to get to the part that is not working properly, so, to transform a mood, we need to be able to dissect it into its component parts. An essential part of this is the overcoming of fear. Most people are frightened by their bad moods. We speak of being in the grip of a mood, overwhelmed, weighed down, burdened by it, or enslaved to it. The Roman Stoic philosopher Epictetus, who was born a slave, claimed that 'men are troubled not so much by things as by their appreciation of things'. As a slave there was much he could not change, but he realized that however unfree he was externally, he was still master of his own thoughts and feelings. We are suggesting

reflection on bad moods takes the terror out of them

that you too can overcome your enslavement to your moods.

The first step then is to overcome the fear of actually looking at your mood, of facing it. Irrational fears – of spiders, heights, crowded places, public speaking – are often based on an inability to look at what you are frightened of. You turn away as though from the Gorgon's head, and in doing so the tiny little spider swells to horrifying proportions. Perseus used his shield as a mirror with which to overcome the Medusa, and the method of reflection on bad moods takes the terror out of them. A good way to overcome fear of spiders is first to look closely at pictures of them, then sit near to one, and eventually to pick one up and let it run harmlessly over your palm. We need to touch our moods and not be frightened of them if we are to begin to befriend them.

But how to do this? It is all too easy to talk about transformation, sitting comfortably and probably feeling all right. It's not so simple when the mood is upon you. This means that a lot of the work of mood transformation takes place when you are feeling fine. This will pay dividends when bad moods strike – like athletes, we need to do a lot of regular training if we are to perform at our best under stress.

Naming the Mood

If you can name and describe how you are feeling that puts a space between you, the one who is doing the describing, and the mood itself. You are beginning to separate yourself from your mood and so to contain it. Part Two of this book consists of accounts of different moods which we hope will stimulate readers to start to talk – to themselves and others – about their moods.

Feeling the Mood

Naming is not the same as feeling. We have to take ourselves by the hand and enter the cave with all its darkness and invisible, creeping nastiness. Lurking there are many fears and memories and painful experiences from the past which colour our present thoughts and feelings. Perhaps an interview was difficult because we carry a message from childhood that we must always 'do well', that we are only loveable if we are successful, that our parents will turn away from our weaknesses and failures. Perhaps we feel so bereft when our grown-up children leave home because it reminds us of the time when our parents split up and we felt so helpless and abandoned. Perhaps we are so angry with our boss when he ignores us because our parents were too busy or preoccupied with their own problems to notice us much as children. We need ways to let these old feelings well up, to face them again, make friends with them, find a place for them in our lives. They are part of our story, and if we can make a story about ourselves we are beginning to put a shape around something that seems chaotic and threatening, to make it manageable, to contain the unruly beasts of our emotions.

Embodying the Mood

We must look at what our moods are doing to our bodies. How is our posture affected? Our breathing? Our heart? Are our jaws clenched with hatred and anger, our muscles floppy with misery and despair? Are we seeing the world through screwed up eyes of hate or fear? Is our voice constricted with suppressed grief? As we become aware of these aspects, we can begin to send different messages to our mind from our body, an important ingredient in emerging from 'bad' moods.

NO 'ARRIVAL'

These methods, although simple, have to be worked at, especially in the initial stages before they have become integrated into our lives. We never simply 'arrive' in a permanent state of equanimity in which bad moods are a thing of the past. Even the most aware or enlightened person has their share of problems and difficult days. There is no simple or instant 'cure' for bad moods, and we should be intensely suspicious of anything that claims to be one. Life itself is a continuous struggle between construction and destruction, between the forces of growth and those of decay. It is a mistake to equate 'good' with growth and life, 'bad' with dissolution and death. Life and death are inextricably intertwined. They are as interdependent as day and night. It is the same with moods. Good moods do not last for ever – clinging onto them at all costs often accelerates their disappearance. Similarly, if we can begin to see that bad moods are not really 'bad', just a necessary, an inevitable part of living, messages we need to hear, that there is no joy without suffering, no intimacy without aloneness – then we shall have made a small step towards the miraculous paradox of transformation, which can be called reparation or resurrection, which lies at the heart of our being.

SUMMARY

- Choose to master (or mistress) your moods rather than continue to be dominated by them.
- You may not be able to control many external events, but you can control your reactions to anything and everything.
- Unravel the meaning of your moods.
- Develop your inner parent who will protect your inner child.
- Allow your moods to have a fair hearing and treat them with respect.
- Value your moods – they are the mirror of your hidden self.

CHAPTER 4
HOW TO BE A MOOD-TRAVELLER: THE MOOD TRANSFORMATION METHOD

'…emotion recollected in tranquillity: emotion is contemplated until the tranquillity gradually disappears and an emotion does itself actually exist in the mind. In this mood successful composition begins…'

(Wordsworth)

Sailors have two kinds of problem: either there is no wind and they can't get out of harbour, or the winds are so strong they are likely to founder. So too with moods: they may be 'blocked', in which case the sufferer feels 'nothing' and yet is deeply unhappy, or they may blow up into an emotional storm, which rages so fiercely that the person affected feels in danger of drowning.

In this chapter we look at ways of transforming 'bad' moods by staying with them rather than avoiding them. Although the sailor does very different things depending on whether he is becalmed or in a storm, the mood-traveller can use the same method with both blocked and out-of-control emotions. In both cases feelings have first to be gathered up so that you can hold them and contemplate their true nature. As 'bad' moods they are scattered in a sea of fear or rage, or locked away away inside the self. Before beginning to transform your moods you need to find some inner peace. Controlled breathing and relaxation can give you the tranquillity you need to tackle your moods.

ACHIEVING TRANQUILLITY

Breathing

Breathing is the most essential and primal of all human activ-
ities. The baby's first breath is the start of life as a separate
being. The flow of breath in and out of our lungs is a rhythm as
basic as the heart beat – as you slow the breath so you slow
the heart rate. Breathing connects us intimately with the world
around us. There is a strong link between breathing and the
emotions: fear, anger and excitement all manifest themselves
through changes in breathing. Watching over a troubled or ill
person, we see them gradually relax as the slow, regular,
measured breath of sleep begins to take over, and, as it does
so, we too begin to breathe more easily. Breathing in time with
another person, we share their experience. We need to learn
to treat our troubled selves in the same way. The two-way traffic between mind and body makes breathing a powerful
method of influencing emotions. Becoming aware of the
breath and focussing on it has a calming and centring effect
on our whole being.

Exercise: *Learning to breathe*

To practise the calming effect of breathing, sit or lie in a
quiet room comfortably supported on pillows or cushions
so you feel no strain. Keep your back straight to open
your chest. Make sure you are warm enough and will not
be disturbed. Close your eyes and put your hand above
your navel. Take in a long, even breath slowly. Feel your
hand rise. Relax all tension. Pause. Breathe out slowly and
fully. Avoid making an effort. 'Watch' the breath coming in
and out at your nostrils. If you are gulping or gasping, alter
the breath so it is smooth and silent and easy. The even
tick of a clock may make it easier to regulate the breath.
After ten measured inhalations and exhalations let the

---

body continue at its own pace. Keep the hand in touch with the abdomen for a few more breaths, feeling it rise and fall. Watch out for tension in your muscles and, if you notice any, let it go. Imagine all strain and tension being absorbed into the ground beneath you. Continue to 'watch' the breath throughout the practice. It can be helpful to concentrate on a word or phrase as you do so – it may be simply 'in... out', 'peace... ease' or one of your own choosing. Another useful method is to count the breaths from one to five and back to one again, counting on the out-breath: 'in...one, in...two, in...three, in...four, in...five, in...one' and so on.

Do this breathing practice for a short period each day, starting, say, with five minutes and building up to ten, fifteen or twenty if you like. It will get gradually easier as you go along. You will soon start to look forward to your few minutes of peace and concentration, and to feel uneasy if circumstances mean you have to forgo it. Make it a part of you daily routine. You will feel

> *You will feel refreshed and relaxed after after a period of breath-watching*

refreshed and relaxed after a period of breath-watching. As you are doing it you will find that thoughts, images, ideas come into your mind. Plans, regrets, worries, memories, hopes, fantasies will appear. Try neither to follow these, nor to banish them from your mind, just accept them for what they are, acknowledging them but not becoming bogged down in them. If you are worrying about something, observe 'Anxious thoughts are arising in me...' All the time try to return to your breathing and to focus your attention loosely on it.

The more practised you become at breathing, the more you

can use it at odd moments during the day – while you are driving your car, or waiting for a bus or for the kettle to boil. As you start to become aware of your breathing in this way, 'boring' situations, such as waiting at traffic lights and in doctors' waiting rooms, or interminable meetings can be opportunities to practise your relaxing and breathing technique and also alleviate anxiety or irritation. Neutral or even unpleasant situations become transformed into positive opportunities. You need only watch your breath for a minute or two, but it can help to bring you back to yourself, to calm and focus your thoughts. It is a basic method for loosening the grip that a bad mood can have on your body: when you are stressed or anxious always try to breathe calmly. Becoming aware of your breathing restores the balance and flow between body and mind, inner and outer, self and the environment, that become blocked and disrupted by bad moods.

Relaxation

Breathing and relaxation go naturally together. Relaxation helps you to concentrate on your breathing; deep breathing is an important part of relaxation. Start by trying to become aware of how unrelaxed you are for much of the time. As you go about your normal routines, focus on the musculature of your body. If you are walking along, how stiff are your trunk and upper limbs? Do you need all that tension? If you are having lunch at work, are you wolfing your food down, your body stiff and your posture awkward, ready to rush off to your next appointment? How relaxed are you as you lie in bed even ?

Exercise: Learning to relax

Set aside a few minutes in the day for total relaxation. This can be done either sitting or lying. Lie on the floor with your back straight, your legs loosely falling apart, with a cushion under your knees if it feels more comfort-

---

able, your palms facing upwards, your eyes closed. Or, if you prefer, sit comfortably in a chair with your legs uncrossed and your back straight and eyes closed. Make sure you are warm enough. For most of us sitting takes up so much of our day that it is good to cultivate a relaxed posture. Now focus systematically on the different muscles of your body, starting with the feet and working gradually up the body until you end with the face muscles. In your mind test how tense they are. Then deliberately make them as tense as you can for a second or two. Then let all the tension go, relax them completely, feel the stiffness draining away like electricity earthing itself. Say to yourself, 'I am fully relaxing my feet…legs…bottom…back…shoulders…forearms…wrists…hands…fingers, etc.' As you do so, focus on each part in turn and let go all tension. Picture some warm safe and pleasant place where you are lying in full relaxation – a sunny beach or a feather bed for example. As you do this, try to breathe deeply and with awareness.

Just as breathing links us up with our surroundings, so gravity holds us to the ground, rooting and earthing us in a way that reminds us of our connections with our environment, how we have come from the earth and will return to it. Again, as with breathing, you can practise relaxation on many occasions during the day, especially if a bad mood is dogging you. Become aware of tension and distortion in your posture and try to return to your relaxed, alert, upright, balanced position.

TRANSFORMATION

Breathing and relaxation help in two ways to start the process of mood transformation. First, they provide much needed tranquillity. Second, they help to gather your feelings so that you begin to become aware of them. As you relax and breathe, your suppressed and buried moods start to come into awareness. By bringing you back to yourself they help to focus all the fears and feelings that you have scattered into your environment. You start to own your feelings. You see that the anger you feel towards your neighbour, boss or partner, although stimulated by him, belongs to you and can only be altered by you.

Mood-Brooding

Breathing and relaxation enable you to control and contain your feelings. The next step is to hold onto them, to contemplate them in your mind's eye. We call this mood-brooding. A 'broody' hen withdraws herself from the flock and spends her time sitting on her eggs until they hatch, when she becomes a very busy and involved mother. Similarly we all need to 'brood' at times – to withdraw into ourselves, to have periods of tranquil contemplation. Out of this brooding can come new life and a new engagement with the world. Most people allow themselves moments of meditative withdrawal from time to time: while washing-up, lying in the bath, fishing, walking or just 'doing nothing'. Mood-brooding encourages you to extend these moments of contemplation, to value them, and to make them a regular part of your life.

we all need to 'brood' at times – to withdraw into ourselves, to have periods of tranquil comtemplation

Mood-brooding can be thought of as a dance with three steps: gather, hold, let go. First you collect and control your feelings by breathing. That brings you back to yourself. Then you hold the image of a mood or emotion in your mind's eye – you are holding it, rather than the other way round. Finally you gradually let go, using inner dialogue and visualization to transform your moods.

Visualisation

Mood-brooding requires you to find a quiet space and some uninterrupted time to be with yourself. If you live in a busy and crowded house you may have to resort to the bathroom! Start with a period of relaxed breathing as we have already described. Now focus your mind on the mood itself – your depression, anger, apathy. As you do so, images and feelings will begin to well up in your mind. From a jumble of images one may begin to emerge more strongly than the others. Probably it will encapsulate whatever it is that is bothering or upsetting you. If you are angry with your husband picture him as vividly as you can in your mind's eye, while continuing to breathe steadily. Look at him from all angles and in all lights – good and bad. If you are worried about one of your children – who is struggling in some way perhaps or not well – again allow a succession of images of your child to pass across your mind. See them in their suffering, perhaps breathless with asthma; see them playing and running freely and happily; see them as they were as a baby; picture them in the future, a parent like yourself; imagine them before they were born and after you and they are dead. All the time hold the image that your mood conjures up steadily in your mind. However horrible or painful the image, it is safely contained within a protective shell of tranquil breathing and relaxed posture.

The Good
Internal Parent

Once the images have arisen in your mind you can then gently shape and alter them with the help of creative day-dreaming and inner dialogue. Your 'bad' mood can be thought of

> The Mood Transformation Method is based on the normal way in which parents help their children to get over bad feelings

as a frightened or angry or sad child. The Mood Transformation Method is based on the normal way in which parents help their children to get over bad feelings and to mourn the everyday losses and miseries of life. It helps, as Freud put it, 'turn neurosis into ordinary human misery'! To do this you need to find and cultivate a good internal parent who will do inside yourself what was done, or should have been done, for you as a child. Your 'bad' moods may connect with a 'bad' parent who failed to nurture or protect you – your good parent will shield the vulnerable child in you from this destructive aspect, and perhaps help you come to terms with the child-like part of this 'neglectful' parent who was unable to look after you properly.

Creative Day-Dreaming and Inner Dialogue
In creative day-dreaming the good internal parent helps you to take the image which presents itself to your imagination, to understand it and gently to alter it so that true feelings emerge from a jumble of anxiety and confusion.

EXAMPLE: FINDING A SON'S ANGER THROUGH CREATIVE DAY-DREAMING

Peter had split up with his first wife when his son Sam was 5, but had maintained regular contact with him over the subsequent years. In due course he remarried and had two daughters by his second wife. Sam came to stay regularly and got on well with his half-sisters and reasonably amicably with his stepmother, although there were occasional tensions. But as Sam entered adolescence things began to deteriorate, and his visits became more and more strained. Normally chatty and outgoing, Sam became withdrawn and uncommunicative. His school performance, previously good, fell off. Things came to a head during a summer holiday in a rather cramped rented cottage in which Sam joined the family for two weeks – much longer than his usual visits. He was silent and refused to participate. His stepmother became angry and exasperated. Peter was increasingly worried and guilty. He felt angry with Sam but guiltily did not want to 'spoil' his brief stay with unpleasantness.

Using the Mood Transformation Method he brooded on Sam. He saw the cheerful attractive boy he used to be. He saw him now – sullen and silent, his long hair hiding his normally friendly features. He painfully remembered Sam's sadness at the time of the divorce, and the many illnesses he had around that time that seemed to linger for weeks on end. He recalled his own adolescence – filled with frustration and unexpressed anger. He brought his thoughts back to Sam and suddenly saw what had been staring him in the face. He pictured Sam, fists clenched, so filled with rage that he could not speak. He saw for the first time that Sam was furiously angry with him for having 'abandoned' him, for remarrying, for replacing him with two daughters, for expecting him to accept everything that had happened without protest. Once that picture had emerged he saw in his mind's eye Sam sweep back his hair and look straight at him. He felt a sense of relief and resolution. Later, while he and Sam were walking together, Sam suddenly started to reveal some of his discontent and fury. Peter stood his ground on some points, but also acknowledged the depth and reality of Sam's feelings. Father and son cried and embraced, and, with the air at least partially cleared, Sam became more forthcoming, Peter firmer and less guilt-ridden.

Combining 'inner dialogue' with creative day-dreaming is another way in which your good internal parent can reach and transform difficult emotions. Once you have formed an image through visualization, hear yourself saying some gentle words to your inner child. See how the child responds so that conversation and transformation begins to take place inside your imagination. You may see your sadness in the form of a weeping child within you. Hug her, comfort her, hold her and reassure her that all will be well, just as you would do with with your own child who woke in the night from a terrifying nightmare – say: 'You'll be all right. I'll look after you'. If you see your temper as a violent storm at sea, watch as the force of the wind and waves abates and exhausts itself as they pound onto the rocks and eventually subside. If your hatred and jealousy is a venomous snake, stand back with caution and in your mind gradually start to play on your pipe until the serpent is charmed and comes under your control. Always aim to contain and hold the 'bad' emotions, to separate the observing self from the feeling, to carry out mental 'experiments' in which you alter the emotion into a less dominating form, drawing its sting. Through inner dialogue you will develop a conversation with your mood. 'Hello anger. What are you trying to tell me? What are you going to throw at me next ?' By using your non-angry self to have a conversation with the angry part of you, you start to create a more equable inner world in which hatred is balanced by love, fury by calm, fear by security.

EXAMPLE:
LISTENING TO THE CHILD WITHIN

Felicity was a 25-year-old woman working as a classroom assistant in a primary school. Attractive, intelligent and creative, she was plagued by mood swings that left her feeling utterly forlorn at times, at others wildly ecstatic as though walking on air. Her father had died when she was 8, and not long afterwards she had been seriously sexually abused by a neighbour. She had not dared tell her grief-stricken mother. In her teens she had started to drink heavily and had entered several unsatisfactory relationships with men. She was now living alone in a bed-sitter near her mother and stepfather, whom she saw occasionally. Things were going reasonably well for her until her best friend, on whom she was very dependent, became engaged. Felicity was filled with contradictory emotions. She felt happy for her friend, but at the same time felt utterly abandoned, jealous and alone. She went out with some acquaintances, got completely drunk, and ended up in bed with someone whom she hardly knew. Feeling desperate, when she got home she tried the Mood Transformation Method. The image she saw most clearly was that of a little lost girl around ten years old. Using inner dialogue she asked the child 'What would you like me to say or do to you ?' 'Hug me, hold me, soothe me, ask me what is wrong,' came the reply. Felicity pictured herself holding the child tightly, stroking her hair, lovingly looking into her face. Although she began to cry, she also felt much calmer. She could face her feelings of jealousy towards her friend and did not, at least for a while, feel the urgent need to rush off into the arms of someone who would momentarily want her, or to blot out her searing feelings of loss with alcohol.

As these examples show, 'bad' feelings are not eliminated by the Mood Transformation Method. Instead, blocked feelings like anger are released in a way that does not feel unbearably threatening, and overwhelming feelings like jealousy and loneliness are held in such a way that they can be borne. The aim is to release the 'pure' authentic feeling that lies within the confusion and fear. Beyond apathy there may be a valid rage, concealed in depression there is a true grief that needs to have its voice heard, behind overexcitement there is a sadness and vulnerability that have been neglected for too long.

Pure grief, anger, sadness – it is hard to say whether these are any less 'good' than joy, excitement, loving kindness. These themes will be expanded when we come to look at the different moods in detail, but first we must consider some other methods that can be helpful in the transformation of 'bad' moods into 'good'.

SUMMARY

- Collect your feelings by breathing and relaxation.
- Hold your feelings by mood-brooding and visualization.
- Transform your feelings by developing your good internal parent and by creative day-dreaming and inner dialogue.

CHAPTER 5
AWARENESS: BREAKING AND
ENTERING YOUR MOODS

'…If the doors of perception were cleansed…' (Blake)

For most of our lives we operate within a narrow range of awareness and with very little focus on the myriad of detail which makes up the world. If we started to think about all the muscles involved in walking we might never get up out of our chair! But when things go wrong it is important to focus on the affected parts, as for example when recovering from an injury or a stroke. Also, this lack of focus means that we often miss some of the beauty and richness of the world around us. If you have ever gone for a country walk with a naturalist, you will have been amazed by the number of birds, insects and plants there are to notice and name and wonder at, many of which you failed to see in your state of unfocused attention.

Awareness enables you to enter your moods, to break the hard shell that surrounds them, to extract their accumulated residues and to release the energy they contain. Developing awareness helps in the transformation of negative feelings. By studying yourself you become an expert instead of the helpless, defeated person you thought you

You will always know more about yourself than anyone else can – if only you will allow the awareness to surface

were. You will always know more about yourself than anyone else can – if only you will allow the awareness to surface. You will find that there is far more to you than you imagined, that your 'bad' parts are balanced by many seeds of competence, hope and generosity which, like the ignorant country walker, you just had not noticed or named.

IDENTIFYING AND DESCRIBING YOUR MOOD

Talking about a problem or a bad feeling to a trusted friend can be tremendously helpful. But all too often the right person just isn't there when we need them, or we feel too embarrassed to burden them, or the moment never seems to arise, or they are telling us about their problems rather than listening to ours. If we can learn to listen to our own inner voice, find our inner guide and teacher, it becomes much easier to approach other people and to trust in their capacity to listen to us. Also, once we feel more confident in being able to tackle our inner world ourselves, we are much more likely to put the help that comes from finding a listening ear to good use.

Exercise: *Finding a word to describe your mood*

A simple exercise will help you to start immediately. Take one or two breaths so that you are aware of yourself rather than what is going on around you. Now allow a word to come into your mind that describes the predominant mood you are in. It may be a pleasant or neutral mood – 'peaceful', 'calm' 'interested' – or an underlying feeling – 'sad', 'confused', 'lonely'. Once the word has emerged, keep it in your mind and, as you go through your day, come back to it from time to time to see what has happened. Has your mood changed? Is it the same but more, or less, intense? Do any images come with the word to illustrate it – if you are lonely perhaps a picture of an isolated house or a windswept icy plain? Note these in your mind. Repeat the exercise every day for a few days.

The Mood Diary

If bad moods persist it is a good idea to keep a 'mood diary', using a notebook and pencil. If you live in a noisy flat or are a parent of small children it may be difficult to find the time and space to do this, but give yourself the right to concentrate exclusively on yourself for a small part of each day. This may mean locking yourself in the bathroom, getting up ten minutes earlier each day, not watching a TV programme you don't really enjoy or not flicking through a magazine or paper that doesn't really interest you!

Exercise: Keeping a mood diary

Go over in your mind your feelings/emotions/moods since you got up today. You may want to start by putting simple words down like 'depressed', 'fed up', 'furious', or 'O.K.', 'not bad', 'nothing to report'. Score your moods on a scale from 0 to 10. Next, try to expand the descriptions by saying what the mood was like. You can start by using conventional phrases: 'depressed as hell', 'like a ton weight', 'miserable as sin', 'walking zombie'. Then try to find your own words and images. Feel the untapped creativity within you. Don't be inhibited or shocked by the violence or exaggeration of your descriptions – 'I'd like to rip his guts out', 'I just want to go to sleep and never wake up', 'I hate everyone and everything' – they are only words, and they're for your eyes only. Try to be vivid in your descriptions in a way that is relevant to you. One farmer's wife described her depression as being like a February day in Devon when it had been raining for weeks on end and she had to wade through the mud to feed the pigs!

Recording 'Automatic Thoughts'

You may want simply to write an account of what has happened (or not happened – why won't that phone ring ?) and how you have reacted emotionally. Here too it can help to be systematic in your recording of your moods, and the way you react to events. Bad moods influence the way we see the world. If we are in a 'bad' mood, when something unwanted or frustrating happens we may respond automatically with a lot of negative thoughts that make us feel even worse. The feelings we have are valid, but they may be accompanied by irrational thoughts which it is helpful to examine and challenge. We tend to 'catastrophize', turning one small event into a global feeling of neglect and despair.

EXAMPLE: THE MISSING BOYFRIEND

Say you are waiting for your boyfriend to ring and he doesn't. Immediately your automatic thoughts may start telling you he doesn't care about you, has got another girlfriend, that nobody has ever cared for you, you'll never get married and so on. You have moved in no time from a molehill to a mountain. You can resist these automatic thoughts by calmly considering alternative explanations. Perhaps the phone is out of order, or he is working late and can't get away. Maybe he is angry with you, but does that necessarily mean the end of the relationship? Even if it does, won't that mean at least you can get back to seeing some of your friends whom you have neglected because you were so wrapped up in him? And so on.

An example of an automatic thoughts chart

Exercise: The flat battery

Divide a sheet of paper into four columns and with headings above each of them: 'event', 'automatic thoughts', 'feelings and actions' and 'alternatives'. Take a particular upsetting event that has happened during the day – say the car has broken down – perhaps the battery is flat. Write that down in the event column. What were your thoughts about it? Were they 'Oh that's the last straw, everything always goes wrong for me', or 'This is a disaster, however are we going to find the money to buy another', or 'It's all my fault for buying a second hand car from that dodgy garage'? Those are the automatic negative thoughts that often spring up when we are low in mood. Fill them in in the 'automatic thoughts' column. Now, what was the mood? Defeated, miserable, depressed, angry or apathetic? What did you do? Sit down and have a cigarette, scoff a snack, ring your partner in tears, shout at the children? Note that under 'feelings and actions'. And now, in a fourth column, you can consider what happened in some tranquillity. Could you have looked at what happened in a different way? Was it really your fault? What would be the best possible way to resolve the problem? For example, to stay calm and ask a friend or neighbour for help.

Humour

An invaluable antidote to bad moods is humour. The release and relaxation of uninhibited laughter is like an oasis in a desert. Some friends will make you laugh – seek them out. Others will find you amusing; this is good for your self-esteem, and they should be cultivated. Some will leave you feeling flat and dull and discontented; they should be avoided when you feel sensitive yourself. One friend who at times suffers from bad moods also finds amusement all around her. One day she produced a plastic

> *An invaluable antidote to bad moods is humour*

bag and, with a deadly serious expression, said 'What about this ?' It contained a carrot with an uncanny resemblance to the bottom half of a rather generously endowed man! She said it had lightened her day, and she had not cooked it because she wanted to share her amusement!

EXAMPLE: SAVED BY THE MARX BROTHERS!

Even when things are tragic they don't have to be solemn. One man was given a few weeks to live by his doctors. He ordered the complete set of Marx Brothers films from the video shop and spent the next twenty-four hours watching them from his deathbed, in fits of laughter. He was still laughing when he came for his check-up appointment twelve months later!

FEELING YOUR MOOD

Mrs Beeton states in her famous recipe for rabbit-pie: 'First catch your rabbit.' First catch your mood, name it, know it. If moods were animals they would be of many types: shy, retiring creatures that live underground like rabbits so that you need agility and sensitivity to catch them, or wild, fearsome beasts like lions that you need courage to face. Moods need to be unblocked, or tamed.

Awareness: Breaking and Entering Your Moods **53**

EXAMPLE: A SUDDEN UNBLOCKING

Paul consulted his doctor with 'tennis elbow' that just would not heal up. In a moment of inspiration (and frustration) the doctor asked him if there was someone he felt angry with and wanted to hit. Suddenly the man slammed his hand down on the table shouting 'Yes, I'm bloody furious with my headmaster'. Power had returned to his arm.

EXAMPLE: RAGE CONTAINED

Dave, a Trades Union representative, was told by his employer that because of falling order books compulsory redundancies were going to be imposed on the workforce. When he remonstrated, the employer said in a sneering voice that since half of the workmen never did a proper day's work anyway they would hardly notice losing their jobs. Filled with rage, the shop steward could not believe his ears. He felt speechless with impotent fury. He left the room for a few minutes and went into the fresh air, where, not without difficulty, he used the breathing techniques to calm himself and see his anger in a more detached way. He saw how his insensitive and beleaguered employer was probably blaming the workforce because of his own financial worries. The shop steward returned to the negotiations, standing his ground without blowing his top. Short-time working was successfully negotiated in place of redundancies.

Making neutral situations into positive ones

1 Enjoy the moment. Use queues to breathe, observe yourself, stand correctly. In your car enjoy red traffic lights: they give you an opportunity to relax and release tensions (see p. 39).

2 Look for the funny side of situations.

3 Mood-brood if you feel bored or blank. Observe what images and thoughts arise.

4 Take ten deep slow breaths. Relax tension in your neck, shoulders and abdomen.

5 When negative thoughts about yourself come into your mind such as 'I am afraid', invent new phrases like 'I am freed'; 'I'm a warrior, not a worrier'.

6 Keep a dream diary. Note the feeling of the dream: fear, excitement, comfort. Your dreams may compensate for what is going on, or not going on, in your life (see p. 58).

7 Write a list of all the aspects of yourself you like least such as greed, impatience, dishonesty. Think about each one and transform them into characteristics you would like to have. Greed could become 'an appetite for life'; impatience 'excitement and eagerness'; dishonesty 'a desire to seem perfect to oneself and others'. Try to find the origins of these attributes. Learn to forgive yourself.

EXPRESSING YOUR MOOD

Once you have identified your mood you can give expression to your feelings. A good way to do this is to write down some of your painful (and happy) memories from the past. Autobiographical writing like this can be very helpful in putting bad feelings to rest.

EXAMPLE: 'DEAR DAD AND MUM...'

Jim, a young man in his twenties, became depressed. He was a foreman in a garage and he had to spend a lot of time ordering men much older than himself about, which he found very difficult. He was happily married, but in his depression became worried by the thought that he might not really love his wife and that he might, without really wanting to, be unfaithful to her. Through mood-brooding Jim remembered how miserable he had been in his teens when his mother had an affair and left home temporarily, and how he felt he had to look after his father who was very unhappy and bad-tempered. This brought up earlier memories of hearing his parents row while he was upstairs in bed, going down to try to stop them and being shouted at for his pains. He began to see how his fears about his own marriage and difficulty with the older men at work might be related to the anger and confusion he had felt then. Describing these feelings in an autobiographical letter to his parents (which was not sent), helped Jim to come to terms with the past and to differentiate it from the present.

Another good way to get in touch with buried or overwhelming emotions is through poetry or painting or music. You may immediately say 'Oh, but I can't draw for toffee...' Don't worry – technical skill is quite irrelevant. Your feelings are yours and you can give expression to them.

Another good way to get in touch with buried or overwhelming emotions is through poetry or painting or music

EXAMPLE: BUTTERFLIES

A little girl with leukaemia drew a grave with herself weeping beside it mourning her own death, all in black and white. Then she filled the sky with brightly coloured butterflies – symbols of regeneration, of life and its ephemeral nature. She then gave herself wings so she could rise above her fear of death.

For some people music will be their favoured mode of expression. If you can play an instrument, try to improvise in a way that expresses how you feel – again, don't worry what the neighbours (or your partner or children) think. This is something you need to do – it could even save your life.

You don't need to be an Ashkenazy or a Clapton. Maybe you just need to make sounds, moan or shout out your feelings. No one will be hurt by them – and they can't be worse than the traffic noise or aeroplane sounds overhead. A good time for moaning or shouting is when you are alone in the car. No one can hear you, so you can really let rip – although other drivers may give you funny looks! Ignore them. It is you that is hurting inside – anything you can do to relieve the pain is worthwhile.

Singing – even if you 'can't' sing – can be tremendously helpful in mood expression and transformation. Collective singing – whether at a football match, in a choir, or just singing along with your favourite blues singers – breaks you out of your island of unhappiness, brings you into contact with the emotions which we all share, helps hold you in the present moment and automatically brings about breath control.

Keeping a Dream Diary

Another route to unblocking or taming feelings is through dreams. Start a dream diary; leave a notebook by your bed and jot down what comes back to you of the night's dreams when you wake up. If you aren't in the habit of remembering your dreams you should not worry as this is true of about half of the population, but you will soon find that dreams do begin to stick in your mind. Try to focus less on the content of dreams, which is often bizarre and hard to follow, more on their emotional message. Was the dream strange or frightening, comforting or blissful? What were the events in the previous day that may have prompted you to dream of them the next night? Where did these emotions originate from, and what is their connection with the things that upset you in everyday life ?

EXAMPLE: THE RED BOX DREAM

Sally was made very unhappy by her husband's unpredictability and moodiness. She dreamed of them carrying a red box together up a steep hill. The box was so large that neither of them could manage it alone. She saw in this hope for the future: together they would carry the treasure and burdens of their relationship. When she talked to her husband about it, they began to collaborate much better with their shared life

---

Things to do when in the grip of a bad mood

1　Think of an animal or image that most nearly fits your mood. Anger could be a volcano or lion, depression a cold, dark cave. Describe it in as much detail as you can.

2　Keep a daily mood chart, scoring your moods from 0 to 10.

3　Write down your most negative and destructive thoughts without shame or self-criticism.

4　Note your responses to difficulty in your diary. 'The boss told me off .' Did you decide to get your revenge on him? Feel helpless and small? Try to reason with him: 'I'm late because…'? Avoid criticizing yourself for your responses. You are a beginner! Think of the way you would like to have handled it and what you would like to have said. Be prepared! It may happen again.

5　Paint or draw how you feel – just use colours or shapes. Enjoy filling the page. Don't worry about artistic skills. You are expressing yourself.

6　Withdraw to a place where you won't be disturbed – the bedroom or bathroom. Put your body in the position that expresses your feelings. If you are very anxious you could crouch like a rabbit and make the noise that seems right: whimper or whine.

Tears

Tears are an almost universal expression of emotion: tears of sadness, shame, relief, fury, exhaustion, joy, elation. From the bereaved at the graveside to the Olympic champion on the

> *From the bereaved at the graveside to the Olympic champion on the rostrum, tears often arise when there are strong feelings*

rostrum, tears often arise when there are strong feelings. There is still a small child within us, for whom tears were one of the earliest ways of expressing feelings and communicating. As you are doing these exercises it is very likely that you will want to weep at some time. Welcome this – the tears release an emotional block, dissolve the lump in your throat. Don't fight them, let them flow. If you can carry them on into strong sobbing, so much the better. They will help ease the pain. They will not last for ever. You may need to cry and seek out a particular bit of music or poetry or film which triggers off tears for you.

Sometimes people want to cry but 'can't'. You may have been told as a child 'Big girls or boys don't cry' or that it is 'babyish' to cry. Tell yourself 'Crying is a human form of expression which is related to feelings, not age', or 'I am a feeling being – I can cry when I want to', or quote George Herbert to yourself: 'Learn weeping and thou shalt regain laughing'. Don't try too hard. Start by noticing the feelings of wanting to cry: a prickling sensation at the back of the throat and eyes, weakness in the legs. Make moaning and whimpering sounds. Lie down with your face in a pillow – very likely the tears will come of their own accord.

PHYSICAL TECHNIQUES OF MOOD TRANSFORMATION

Awareness needs to be extended to the body as well as the mind. As we 'enter' our mood at a physical level we can soothe and reverse its effects on our physical being, so that our mind begins to receive different messages from our body. Being physically fit is also a step towards feeling better. You will also introduce a routine into a day which may seem chaotic. This gives you something positive to do about your mood and that in itself will give you a sense of achievement.

Once again, you need to spend a part of your normal daily life concentrating on yourself. Be generous with yourself – give yourself the attention you need. This is not selfishness or self-indulgence. By giving to yourself in this way you will feel better. The more stable and happy you are, the more you will have to offer others. In the depths of bad moods you often feel neglected or overlooked, that life is passing you by. You are now forced to pay attention to yourself, to become aware of your body and its relation to the world.

Stretching

In the previous chapter we showed how breathing and relaxation develop your awareness of your body while it is at rest. Stretching extends this to the body in motion, developing an awareness of the incredi-

> *Yoga reverses muscular patterns that reflect our predominant feelings and so can be very useful in mood transformation*

ble complexity of our physical frame – the muscles, bones, joints and tendons that hold us up and keep us together. It is beyond the scope of this book to suggest a detailed programme of mindful stretching, and the interested reader is advised to join one of the many Yoga or Tai-Chi classes that are available. Yoga reverses muscular patterns that reflect our predominant feelings and so can be very useful in mood transformation. As your posture becomes straighter, so your feelings start to 'straighten out'. A few exercises each day can, like

> *As your sense of physical balance improves through stretching and exercise, so mental balance will also be restored*

breathing, bring you back to your physical self. The key to mood transformation is a balanced attitude. As your sense of physical balance improves through stretching and exercise, so mental balance will also be restored.

Eating

Eating is a basic bodily function that is powerfully influenced by our moods. Some people lose their appetite when they are miserable; others eat ravenously in an attempt to quell feelings of panic or stave off mental pain. You may swing between the two, and feel guilty about doing so as well. When eating – or not eating – in this way, awareness of food and hunger usually disappears. Someone who 'can't' eat has lost sight of the fact that they need to eat to live, while the gorger is usually unaware of the taste and texture of what they are stuffing into themselves.

Practise becoming aware of the nature of the food you are eating. If it is a simple loaf of bread, think about the field where the wheat was sown, the many human minds and hands that have contributed to the making of the loaf. Think about the positive and negative aspects of the modern food industry: the scientific techniques which have made it possible for you and millions of others to buy fresh wholesome bread wherever you happen to live – but also the pesticides implicated in its production which may be affecting the biosphere, the long, hot, underpaid hours of many bakery workers (compared with the pride and respect of the traditional self-employed baker), and a world economy in which the West is destroying itself with superabundance while in the Third World people are dying from starvation.

These thoughts are not designed to put a puritanical dampener on the pleasures of food. Celebrate and enjoy eating, both for what it is and as a social event. Becoming aware of what you are eating, where it has come from, and why we need food can add to the good feelings that a meal brings, so that eating, especially if shared, becomes a means of recovery from bad moods, rather than a way of trying to escape from them.

Sexuality

Sexuality is a vast area, too vast to be touched on more than superficially, but no book on moods would be complete without at least some mention of it since our sexual life is so closely bound up with our emotions. The principle of awareness applies as strongly to sex as it does to all other aspects of life.

As well as bringing excitement, intense pleasure, relief from tension and relaxation, sex can, if you have a loving partner, give you a wonderful feeling of closeness and a sense of being valued and cared for physically and emotionally.

Because it is so exciting and transporting, sex is often used as a way of distracting oneself from bad moods. Successful men are enormously attractive to women. Beautiful women are irresistible to men. The excitement of the chase, seduction and consummation make a welcome relief from deep feelings of misery or hollowness or lonely isolation. Having an affair alleviates the routine of responsibilities and domestic chores. It may be based on a split between a secret excited self and a bored 'home' self which means that bad feelings are shut away from the light of awareness and cannot be counteracted by good feelings. The excitement of 'illicit' sex may be short-lived, and may well intensify the bad feelings once the brief moment of pleasure or fleeting intimacy has passed.

Acknowledging an affair, perhaps to a neutral person, provides an opportunity to bring our discontent out into the open – and will lessen the compartmentalization of the self, making us feel more integrated and whole.

Awareness is all. Becoming aware of the implications of your sexuality will intensify its pleasures, and make it less likely that you will be driven unwillingly by your sexuality into destructive relationships as a desperate but doomed attempt to overcome bad feelings. It is important to realize how bad moods can all too easily push you into sexual relationships which lead to exploitation and pain.

Exercise

Compared with our parents and grandparents, let alone our evolutionary ancestors, Western men and women lead a very sedentary existence. Regular exercise is not just good as a method of weight reduction, blood pressure control, and as a protection against heart disease, but can also improve depression and help with anxiety. Physical activity gives a feeling of well-being and healthy tiredness which is the antithesis of the heaviness of a miserable mood or the tension of chronic fear. The sense of accomplishment that goes with any physical effort – a flowerbed dug, a park walked round, ten lengths of a swimming bath swum, or a game of badminton won or lost – counteracts the lowering effects of a bad mood and may also stimulate the release of endorphins, which are the brain's natural chemical pain-relievers and mood-elevators and have a direct impact on the mood.

Exercise: On exercise

A good starting point is to become aware of the extent to which you are trapped in a sedentary way of life. Keep a record of how many miles (or fractions of a mile!) you walk in a week, how often you exercise to the point of getting

---

out of breath, and for how long. For fitness, this should happen for twenty minutes two or three times per week. How often do you take an escalator or car where you could walk or bicycle? What is the effect of your lack of exercise on the environment? Could the warm glow that a brisk walk gives save on your transport and heating bills ?

Body and mind

1   Practise breathing. If you can't set aside ten minutes, do it on buses or trains, or while waiting to see people or in the bath (see p. 39).

2   Relaxation. Bring awareness of yourself into yourself. To relax tension, first stiffen the muscle then let it go (see p. 40).

3   Yoga stretching to reverse muscular habits: from 'twisted with anger' to opened and straightened out.

4   Mindful eating. Try to increase your awareness of everything you eat. You are what you eat. Eat slowly and thoughtfully. There is as much pleasure in eating one square of chocolate in small nibbles, letting the sweetness penetrate slowly, as there is in scoffing the whole bar. Think what good the food you are eating will do for you.

5   Mindful sex. Think of your partner and how you can give them pleasure. Avoid the sort of sex that intensifies feelings of alienation and loneliness.

6   Exercise. Try to find an activity you really enjoy. Exercise routines are hard to stick to if they become a boring chore. Swimming, dancing, walking are not only pleasurable in themselves but induce wellbeing, reduce tension and help us sleep better.

'Positive' Daydreaming

'Castles in the air – they're so easy to take refuge in. So easy to build, too.' (Ibsen)

We have bombarded you with a range of different suggestions and exercises in this chapter. We did so because we wanted to give you a feeling of the great variety of approaches you can use to help yourself to feel better. It is very important that you work out for yourself what feels right for you. Some people need total relaxation – others a vigorous game of squash. Anything which works for you is of value. Anything which helps overcome the passivity of bad moods, which gives you a sense of being able to master the mood rather than being dragged down by it, is important. Sometimes it is useful just to think of what you would like to do – you may never get round to it, or it may be impossible, but 'positive daydreaming' widens your horizons and gives you the sense of freedom which you have lost touch with. Making a list of all the things you would like to do, even if you only actually achieve one of them, can be liberating. So castles in the air should not be sneered at – occasional holidays in them are helpful, although they are not to be recommended as permanent abodes!

A bad mood may be a friend in disguise if it leads you to take hold of your life and question its fundamentals. Are you really living as you would like to?

> A *bad mood may be a friend in disguise*

What would you ideally like to do with your life? Do you need to set goals in order to achieve this? Is there some secret ambition or hope you have nurtured but never allowed to blossom? Some person you would like to meet but have been too shy to approach? Do you habitually shut your desires and daydreams out of your consciousness and, in an attempt to damp down bad feelings, lose touch with the good ones too?

As we consider the different moods in turn in Part Two, we shall be directing you to these basic questions. We believe that, if you can face them, they play an essential part in the transformation of your moods.

SUMMARY

- Teach yourself to resist the undermining effects of negative thinking.
- Invent your own mood metaphors – tame your lion, teach your mouse to roar, calm your storm.
- If you can control your breathing, you can control your life.
- A healthy way of life will improve your mental wellbeing.
- Identify your goals – you will have cleared the way to achieving them.

CHAPTER 6
THE BLUE MOODS

DEPRESSION

'…and deep distress has humanised my soul.'

(Wordsworth)

Depression means to be pressed or forced down – down in the dumps, down at mouth, 'down', drear, dull, deadened. Depression sinks us low, takes us towards the dark hole of failure, futility, feebleness. We feel inert; everything is pointless and empty; we are defeated and feel like giving up. Time and purpose come to a standstill. We can't look forward optimistically to the future (like the child who announced he was 'looking backward ' to returning to school), and the past seems to stretch back like an empty wasteland. Misery overwhelms us. We are near to tears for no clear reason, or a thousand reasons.

We toss and turn restlessly but sleep won't come, or we wake suddenly in the night, our mind a turmoil of fear and regret. We feel rotten and worthless. Everything we have done seems like a failure. We go over and over past mistakes and wrong turnings. Why were we so weak or cowardly or blind or stupid? Nothing is ever going to change. Perhaps we would be better off dead. At least this gnawing pain of isolation and misery and failure would end. We feel disconnected from the world, unlovable and incapable of loving. We hate, despise and punish ourselves.

These are extreme feelings. It is not always that bad – just a glass wall or a blanket between us and the world: the film is in black and white (mostly grey fog) not technicolour, jokes aren't funny; food is eaten for survival, not pleasure. We toil through our day and long for bed as an escape – desperate for sleep, but dreading that it may not come. Friends and family seem to avoid us. Perhaps they are frightened of being sucked into our black pit, bitten by our black dog... And yet, how we long for a word of comfort, a friendly hand held out to us without the expectation of anything in return.

At the heart of depression is loss: loss of hope, loss of those we love, loss of good feelings about ourselves and the world, loss of self-esteem and the esteem of others. We

> *At the heart of depression is loss*

can picture a long line of losses reaching back to childhood perhaps, starting with the most recent one that may have tipped us into depression.

The value of depression is that it provides an opportunity to withdraw from the world so that we begin to mourn what we have lost. Depression is painful, but if we allow ourselves to feel the pain, not to be overwhelmed by it, then the wounds begin to heal. Like someone recovering from a broken limb we need to use the pain as a guide to recovery – too much and we will re-open the wound, too little and atrophy will set in. So too with

> *The value of depression is that it provides an opportunity to withdraw from the world so that we begin to mourn what we have lost*

loss. For our feelings to return, we need to exercise our emotions, however painful they are, neither burying them nor succumbing to them. If we can enter the cave of depression and go through the mourning process, then we emerge back into the light of life strengthened and renewed. If we try for ever to escape facing what is lost, clouds of depression will continue to hang over us and the spirits of the past to haunt us.

Suggestions

The first step is to recognize that you are depressed. It is all too easy to attribute your feelings to the weather, a cold, exhaustion, overwork, PMT. We need to listen to our bodies; an unexplained pain, or a constant feeling of lassitude for which no physical cause can be found, may well be the result of depression.

One reason we avoid thinking that we may be depressed is that it seems shameful: it's the weaklings and people who cannot cope who succumb to depression, we tell ourselves. We need to give ourselves permission to be depressed. During the Gulf War soldiers and airmen spoke openly about their fears, describing how many of them found themselves crying uncontrollably for several hours after returning from a mission. We need to take courage from their example – to admit to and touch our depression without feeling ashamed or punitive towards it.

Picture your depression as a small, lost child, hurt and crying, cut off from everyone that it loves. Treat your depression with the same tenderness you would show to such a child. Think what that child needs most: protection, to be soothed, held, wrapped up and placed gently in a safe place, given comforting food and warm drinks. Say: 'You're feeling bad now, but everything will be all right'. What would your child most like to happen? Picture this for yourself, and in your imagination satisfy your heart's desire, however unrealistic this may seem to your rational mind. What would you really like more than anything else in the world? Write a list. Some things may be impossible, but others very simple to achieve: a cup of tea in bed, a morning 'off ', someone to fix that wonky door handle.

EXAMPLE: FROM DEPRESSION TO SADNESS

Miriam became depressed after she split up with her boyfriend, feeling miserable and worthless and unable to study. She longed to cry but couldn't. She was in her early twenties, a college student in her final year studying biology. Her parents had adopted her after many years of marriage, thinking that they were infertile, but soon after she arrived her mother became pregnant with her brother. However scrupulous her parents had been about not favouring their son, Miriam was painfully aware of being 'different', and this had led to some stormy behaviour in her teens so that she had been expelled from several schools. The feeling of not belonging and being unwanted was intensified during her depression. She became preoccupied with the thought of her 'real' mother and of the difference between her biological and social origins. As she brooded on the image of her mother she was overcome with a wave of sadness, seeing a clear image of her mother weeping as she had to give her daughter away for adoption, and of the torment she must have felt in the weeks that followed. In her mind she pictured a meeting with her mother, saw herself embracing her and telling her that she understood her agony, that everything was all right and was forgiven. She began at last to cry. Gradually her depression lifted, and she returned to college.

Using your mood diary (see p. 50), begin to see how your moods vary through the day – sometimes you can even feel quite good! Using your automatic thoughts chart, look at the way depression colours your perception of things and try to develop alternative, less depressed ways of thinking and reacting.

Set yourself simple tasks which you know you can achieve: washing up slowly and carefully, tidying a chest of drawers or your workshop, sweeping the floor, writing a short note to a friend. Throw away things you no longer need: 'clearing' mentally and literally. Whatever you do, do it attentively and deliberately, not in a rush, thinking always about the task itself: 'Sweeping the floor I know that I am sweeping the floor'. Be aware of your breathing as you sweep. Make simple actions into pleasurable undertakings. Develop a gentle and positive attitude to the job and to yourself for doing it: 'I will sweep this floor as though for a king or queen. I myself am that king or queen who deserves to walk on a floor cleaned with attentiveness'. As you begin to feel better, you will want to show the same consideration to others and will find depths of generosity, helpfulness and compassion in yourself that you were unaware of before.

When you are ready, try to focus on the loss or losses that may lie behind your depressed mood. If it is because someone has died, find a photograph of them and try to look intently at it if possible without regret or yearning, absorbing that person into yourself. Remember a happy or funny moment which you shared, and treasure it. Talk to them, tell them what you are feeling, however 'bad' it may seem. Perhaps you feel very angry with them for leaving you. Tell them so, don't hold back. Picture them alive again, hold them and hug them, tell them: 'I miss you so much. We did have so many good times together'. When you are ready, gently disengage yourself. Let them go.

It sometimes helps to write a letter to some one you have lost, whether by death or because your relationship has broken down.

EXAMPLE: GRIEF AND THE LETTER

Jenny's husband had died suddenly from a heart attack at the age of thirty while playing cricket one Saturday afternoon. She was left with two small boys aged one and three. Ten years later, she began to develop severe neck pains. These were extensively investigated but no physical cause was found. Using the Mood Transformation Method she started to think about her dead husband, and how she had never really had time to grieve for him – she just 'got on with it', finding a job and bringing up the boys. But now they didn't need her so much; what they did need was a father, someone to play cricket with. 'How dare you go and die like that!' she suddenly felt. She sat down and wrote a letter to him, telling him not only about her anger, but also about how much she missed him and needed his help with bringing up their adolescent sons. By the time she had finished writing it she was crying properly for the first time in years – and the neck pains had disappeared!

The expression 'get in touch with' your depression, your anger, your tears should be taken literally. Picture your depressed self and in your mind's eye give yourself the touching and stroking you need. Touch your pain and feel the anger rise up in you just as if someone had bumped into a sore place on your body. Allow yourself to feel angry about everything that has gone wrong, and those who have let you down. Don't be afraid of your tears. If you find it difficult to cry, picture your tears – perhaps locked away in a flask buried deep in the earth. Start to unearth your feelings. When your tears do come, as they will, often unexpectedly, welcome the relief they bring.

Transformation
'The healing power of mourning changes my depression into the pure sadness of loss.'

APATHY

'How weary, stale, flat and unprofitable
Seem to me all the uses of this world!' (*Hamlet*)

The Russians have a special name for someone who lies in bed all day: he is an *Oblomov*. Oblomov was the hero of a novel by Goncharov, and his apathy was a protest against the conventions of 19th-century Russian bourgeois society. He could find no valid reason to get up in the morning; everything was artificial, pointless and boring.

In apathy we lose all motivation. Our battery has gone flat. Merely to crawl out of bed and stagger across the room to make a cup of tea seems like a major expedition. To feel apathetic is to be flattened, heavy, with no inclination to initiate or do anything.

At its worst, apathy is the end result of oppression or torture. Prisoners, especially if kept in inhumane conditions, are often listless and apathetic, as are children subjected to severe forms of neglect or abuse. It is safer to feel nothing than to continue to endure pain and despair day after day, or to face the consequences of our anger (Oblomov was really absolutely furious that no one saw him as special or different). Apathy is a purgatory adjacent to the hell of impotent rage or fruitless despair.

Brief and less malignant forms of apathy are common, especially in adolescence: they reflect feelings of hopelessness about the future and the fear of failure that sometimes thwarts our efforts to achieve happiness or success. Repeated losses or setbacks in adult life may induce a state of partial apathy or 'learned helplessness'. Temporary retreats into apathy are common when the stresses or demands of life overwhelm one. Apathy is a form of non-violent protest. You

> **Apathy is a form of non-violent protest**

'go limp' as a way out of a situation in which you feel controlled by some external force – which may be no more than strong parental expectations of success – which you can neither satisfy, nor openly reject because you are not yet strong enough to find your own direction in life.

Suggestions

In apathy the flow of feeling has been dammed in order to avoid painful feelings of pain or emptiness or fear. Transforming apathy means unblocking the channels of emotion, and this has to be done gently and with tact. The more you try to force yourself to act or feel, the more you will cling to your apathetic state.

It is a good idea to start by thinking about the positive aspects of apathy. For the ancient Greeks to be 'a-pathetic' (without feelings) was a desirable state because it meant one was no longer prey to dangerous emotion. The poet Keats described his creative trances as states of 'negative capability' in which he aimed just to be, without trying to feel or accomplish anything. He found that poetic ideas would spontaneously come to him in such states of reverie or inactive receptiveness.

out of apathy comes some new direction or plan

In the Viking long-houses of the eighth and ninth centuries men tolerated the 'ash-eaters', indolent youths who spent long months lying in front of the fire doing nothing. It was accepted that if left to themselves these exhausted adolescents would eventually become productive members of society. Although in apathy 'nothing' is apparently going on, often out of apathy comes some new direction or plan. You should, at least for a time, stay with your apathy and resist the well-meant efforts of your family and friends to shake you out of it. It is a mistake to dig up a germinating seed or wake a hibernating hedgehog.

Behind your apathy you may be feeling defeated or furious with the world. The apathy reflects a hopeless despair about your capacity to be effective in any way. Mood-brood your apathy – picture it as a miserable and frightened child, a huge doll that has to be carried around, a puppet with no spontaneity of its own other than the capacity to resist having its strings pulled. Look behind the apathy to the anger or fear or unhappiness. In the safety of your brooding, allow yourself to feel those simple and valid emotions. Where are they directed? Who are you punishing with your apathy – parents, spouse, the world? What would you really like to do, and to whom?

Small achievements, like making a cup of tea or going for a walk, can be an excuse for celebration: these small successes may be the first indications of release from the prison of apathy, rather as the escaping prisoner pulls first on a thin cord to which is attached the rope with which he will climb to his freedom.

Transformation
'In apathy I incubate my strength until I am ready to emerge with the courage to make my own choices in life.'

BOREDOM

'Boredom: the desire for desires.' (Tolstoy)

Boredom often appears to be imposed from outside. We complain about a boring meeting, film, or person. We feel trapped in an unstimulating situation from which we cannot escape. Children, who have much less control over their lives than adults, are particularly prone to complain of boredom: 'How was school today ?' – 'Boring'; 'How was your weekend ?' – 'Pretty boring, nothing much happened'. In these everyday examples of boredom, the feeling evaporates almost at once when the boring experience is over: 'Goodness that was boring!' we say, as though to expel the feeling from our system.

But sometimes the boredom persists. In an insidious way it has entered our system. We feel marooned, stuck in a wasteland, caught in a maze from which there seems to be no way out. Everything is dull and stale; we can't breathe properly; we long to throw open the window, but it is stuck fast. We try to read, but the words stay sullenly on the page. We switch on the TV, but it all seems tawdry and artificial. Our family and friends appear predictable and insufferable: we've heard their little puns and stories a thousand times. 'If he tells that joke one more time I think I'll scream', we think to ourselves. But we never do: we just stay stuck with a stifling feeling of boredom and trappedness.

In childhood boredom often has to do with minor forms of abandonment. The child who feels deprived of attention, whose parents are physically present but emotionally absent, may suffer from terrible pangs of boredom. Like grief, there is an emptiness about boredom, a space hollowed out inside you – bored into you – that longs to be filled. Like grief, it often has an accusatory quality: 'Why doesn't someone take some notice of me ?' A woman who had for years felt neglected and belittled by her husband, suddenly burst out to him in a rage: 'I'm intellectually, socially and sexually bored by you'.

Suggestions

Respect your boredom. Like the dark side of the moon, it contains the shadow of your creative self. It is a mark of your free spirit wanting to soar beyond the confines of the everyday. In some circles boredom is almost raised to an art form. Many of the characters in Chekov's plays – minor landowners in fin-de-siècle Russia – are afflicted by a delicious ennui that partly reflects the fate that awaits their doomed

> *Respect your boredom, it contains the shadow of your creative self*

class, but is also an awareness of the indifference of the universe to the petty hopes and fears of mankind.

Think of your boredom as an accusation. By whom do you feel abandoned or let down? Perhaps as a child you felt understimulated when your parents were bogged down in their work or distracted by worries. Using inner dialogue, imagine yourself trying to get their attention. You may have to shout or scream to get them to listen to you. Turn your boredom into anger. 'How dare you neglect me like this!' You will immediately feel better. It may be that the person you are angry with also feels trapped and bored. Perhaps you can release both of you.

EXAMPLE: IN BED BY SIX!

Lucy's depression was dominated by feelings of boredom. She was in her early thirties and felt stuck at home with two small children while her reliable, but predictable, husband worked long hours as a lorry driver. She avoided friends as she felt she would have nothing interesting to say to them. She kept her house immaculate, although she disliked housework intensely. Secretly she wrote poetry expressing her self-hatred and her loathing for the world and her conventional existence. Her parents had run a guest-house and were always busy during her childhood. She was expected to help with the chores from an early age. When she was 11 her parents split up and both remarried. She stayed with her mother who, she remembered, insisted that she went to bed at six so that she could spend time with her new husband who resented Lucy's intrusions. She recalled many hours of boredom stuck in her room with nothing to do and unable to sleep. Eventually she wrote an angry letter to her mother describing these unhappy times from childhood. Her mother was very upset and refused to speak to her for several weeks, but eventually they met amid anger and tears – and were reconciled. Her mother spoke of her feelings of guilt and how torn she was between her daughter and her new husband. Lucy came to accept that things were not as bad as she had remembered all the time, and recalled happy family holidays. When her depression improved, she put more energy into her relationship with her husband, he changed to a less time-consuming job, and they began to have more enjoyable times together.

Picture your boredom as a prison. What do you need to escape: a flute to charm the guards? Money? A gun? Who could help you with your escape plans? If you felt trapped and bored at home, was there an aunt or grandmother who really cared about you and provided fun and laughter? Humour is the great antidote to boredom. Go to any length to find someone or something that will amuse you: a funny novel or video, a friend who can be guaranteed to make you laugh.

Use your breathing to banish boredom. Breathe in freshness and vitality, breathe out staleness and stasis. In any situation, however dull, there are stirrings of life for you to appreciate and explore. Study the other people waiting at the bus-stop, imagine what their lives are like, where they have come from, where they are going to. Strike up a conversation with them. You may even be grateful for the delayed bus. Boredom is expectant, looking for an exciting future that never comes.

> Use your breathing to banish boredom. Breathe in freshness and vitality, breathe out staleness and stasis.

Boredom is timid. It hovers on the fringes of things. You may fail to get involved with an event for fear of rejection, and so find it unstimulating. Take control of your life. You don't have to go to that party if you don't want to, and if you do go, you don't have to wait to be introduced to that interesting-looking man – go up to him and introduce yourself. He may have been as bored as you were – until you get talking. Disclose your feelings: 'I feel shy and awkward not knowing anyone'. Perhaps you are afraid that you are boring? You are not – no one who expresses themselves authentically can be boring. But you may be so paralysed by anxiety that you stifle your creativity. Stifle? Breathe out your boredom. Feel the cold air come into your lungs renewing you and releasing you. As long as we can breathe we are never totally imprisoned.

Transformation
'From boredom to authentic feelings of anger or sadness. From wishing myself elsewhere to living in the present.'

DISAPPOINTMENT

'One cloud is enough to eclipse the whole sun.'
(Thomas Fuller)

Dis-appointment: the expected meeting that never happens. Your hopes and expectations are aroused – then dashed by non-fulfilment. No one can say they have never been disap-pointed: the longed-for letter that never came, the friend who failed to turn up, the lover who let you down, the exam results that were not so good, the team that lost, the birthday present that was forgotten, the pregnancy that failed to progress, the meal that wasn't prepared.

Some people seem to take disappointment in their stride: a short-lived period of unhappiness perhaps, a brief moment of protest, a night out to drown their sorrows and they are back to normal. For others the hollow ache of non-fulfilment lingers, as they endlessly examine what went wrong, or torture themselves with feelings of worthlessness and insignificance. Others switch off their feelings altogether, pretending to themselves that they 'don't really mind' or 'it doesn't really matter', or, worse still, suppress all hope and expectation as a way of avoiding the pain of being let down.

Difficulty in coping with disappointment has its roots in childhood. One of the many tasks of parenthood is to help children through the inevitable disappointments of life. You aren't picked for the school team, your best friend drops you, you fail to get on the course you set your heart on, you arrange to meet someone in town and they fail to turn up – if you feel loved and accepted, that your parents' support is there however good or bad, nice or nasty you are, then you have a basis for coping with difficulty. But the very people who have the power to help you through your setbacks and losses may have been those who exposed you to them. If your parents dismissed your childish miseries as self-indulgence and told you to 'get on with it', or were ill or absent when you needed them, or lectured, moralized and belittled you, you may grow up with the low self-esteem which leads you to expect disappointment. Alternatively, they may have rushed in with reassurance, telling you how wonderful you were and blaming the examiners or whoever it was that let you down, without allowing you to feel and recover from the pain of dashed hopes for yourself.

EXAMPLE: TERRIFIED OF GRIEF

Evan's parents could not bear to see him upset. When they came home to find the TV set had been stolen, Evan, who was nine, was inconsolable at the thought of missing his favourite programme that afternoon. His mother went immediately to buy a new set. When, a year later, the faithful family dog died at the age of 18, Evan's father tried to stifle his son's misery by bringing home a new puppy that afternoon. But Evan could not really enjoy his new pet yet – he was still missing the old one too much.

'Hope springs eternal in the human breast' – desires and longings arise continuously, and, if grief is not allowed to run its course, there may be an endless cycle of raised hopes and dashed expectations.

Suggestions

Be grateful to your disappointment. From it you come to a better understanding of your strengths and limitations. It puts you in touch with reality. Even the plans of great leaders and politicians can come to nothing. From disappointment we learn how our hopes and desires underestimate the difficulty and transience of life.

Mood-brood on your disappointment. Try to picture the hurt child that felt let down and lost. What did he or she truly want? Was it really that job or brilliant A-Level result – or was it a feeling of being competent and 'good enough'? Perhaps there is anger behind your feelings of disappointment. Who is this directed at? Is it really the appointments committee or the examiners, or is it someone from your past? Put this into words, using 'I' statements: 'I feel undervalued and uncared for…'; 'I feel you are far too busy to take much notice of me…'

Come back to the present, to yourself now. Disappointment takes you away from yourself into an imagined future that has been snatched from you. Happiness is now. You feel let down, but the sun still shines, the plants grow, the birds sing. They may seem indifferent to your misery, but you are part of them, of a cycle of nature in which there is a constant balance between growth and decay and rebirth. There is much that is good about you. Make an inventory of your positive qualities. You may not have backed the right horse, but you make a mean pancake, can grow prize-winning leeks and are a wizard at cheering up howling babies. You don't have to hazard your happiness in this way. You can learn to 'meet with triumph and disaster and treat those two imposters just the same'.

Transformation
'In my disappointment I reassess my capabilities and accept reality.'

GUILT

'That is the bitterest of all – to wear the yoke of our own wrongdoing ... One who has committed irremediable errors may be scourged by that consciousness into a higher course than is common ... Feeling what it is to have spoiled one life may well make us long to save other lives from being spoiled.' (George Eliot)

When we feel guilty there is something inside that needs to come out. Guilt gnaws at our insides like a hungry animal. Guilt longs to be set free, to escape from the secrecy and darkness of concealment. We are tormented by pangs of conscience as we picture

> *When we feel guilty there is something inside that needs to come out*

our real or imagined misdeeds. We long to undo what we have done, to be absolved of our crime, to do penance and be forgiven. The murderer returns to the scene of his crime; the guilty husband lavishes bunches of flowers on his betrayed wife.

As so often in 'bad' moods, in guilt we inflict pain upon ourselves in the hope of remaining in control. If we 'confess', we throw ourselves on the mercy of those whom we believe we have harmed, we run the risk of their abandoning us or retaliating in ways which we can do nothing about. By the pre-emptive punishment of guilt we are hoping to assuage their wrath and so maintain our attachment to them. It as though we are saying: 'You can't possibly hurt me more than I am already hurting myself with my guilt'.

There are three types of guilt –
- Authentic remorse or 'good guilt',
- Excessive guilt, and
- Hidden or absent guilt.

Authentic guilt is an important component of close relationships. Our guilt reminds us that our 'selfish' and childlike desires may have damaging consequences for those whom we love. Guilt brings us up short, reminding us that the person we hate and wish to harm is often the very person we love and want to protect. A degree of 'good guilt' is a useful regulator of close relationships whether between parent and child, lovers, spouses or even close friends. Guilt can help you to recognize imperfections – meanness, jealousy, possessiveness – and how hurtful they can be. Guilt helps you to say you are sorry and ask for forgiveness, to show genuine remorse in facing the pain that has been inflicted and to make amends.

'Good guilt' is an important spur towards making things better. If we shout at someone without good reason, our guilt may help us to apologize and try to do better next time. If we

> *'Good guilt' is an important spur towards making things better*

deceive our partner financially or sexually, a sense of guilt may eventually bring things out into the open so that they can be dealt with and resolved. Guilt is in this way a guardian of truth and security.

But guilt, if excessive, can immobilize and constrict. The guilty person tortures himself unnecessarily, heaping blame on himself for the most trivial misdemeanours or holding himself responsible for things which could not possibly be his fault. His weaknesses are mercilessly attacked by a ravaging conscience.

He feels personally responsible for all the poverty and inequality in the world, for every unavoidable accident which has befallen his family. He feels unworthy of existence and may, *in extremis*, feel his only just punishment is death.

People burdened by excessive guilt are over-sensitive to the needs of others. By contrast, those who are incapable of experiencing guilt (sometimes called psychopaths) are at a great disadvantage because, being unable to put themselves in another person's shoes, they cannot picture in their minds the effects of their actions. As a result their relationships tend to be shallow and short-lived, or maintained by coercion rather than mutual consent.

The ability to experience 'good guilt' comes from a childhood which contains a balance between firmness and tolerance. A child needs to feel that his 'bad' impulses and actions are recognized and accepted, not ignored, condoned or unreasonably punished. 'The punishment must fit the crime', not in the sense of an eye for an eye and a tooth for a tooth, but with a real recognition of the pain that we can inflict upon one another, and that, if faced, the pain will be relieved and can be forgiven and forgotten.

EXAMPLE: BROUGHT UP 'BY HAND'

Some children grow up feeling guilty for their very existence. Here is Charles Dickens's account of the guilt imposed on Pip in *Great Expectations* by his ever-complaining sister who brought him up 'by hand': 'She entered on a fearful catalogue of all the illnesses I had been guilty of, and all the acts of sleeplessness I had committed, and all the high places I had tumbled from, and all the low places I had tumbled into, and all the injuries I had done myself, and all the times she had wished me in my grave, and I had obstinately refused to go there.'

Suggestions

The first step is to recognize your guilt, bring it into the light of day, examine it from all sides. How much real harm has been done by your actions? Did you intend to hurt, or was it more an act of thoughtlessness? Does your self-inflicted punishment fit the crime, or are you sadistically condemning yourself for a minor misdemeanour? Can you put things to rights, discuss openly what happened with those whom you have hurt or offended ?

Mood-brood on the part of you that committed the guilty act. Start with something very trivial in which the only person you have hurt is yourself. Let us say you are on a diet and have had a minor lapse and are now filled with remorse. Picture the greedy, deprived part of you that guzzled the cream cakes. So you felt like the knave of hearts for a while – was that really such a crime? Perhaps you have been too stringent in your diet, setting yourself unrealizable goals. Perhaps you need to allow yourself an occasional indulgence. Perhaps the whole idea of a diet was a punishment to yourself for being so 'fat', where 'fat' really equals 'bad'. Perhaps you, like Pip, never felt quite 'right' as a child, never felt fully accepted for what you were, warts and all. Picture this unacceptable part of yourself, say: 'Those cakes were irresistible. I wanted them more than anything. I felt so empty inside'. If you are guilty, it is for not giving yourself the respect and care which you deserve, and for not recognizing that there is a wild, selfish, hungry creature inside you that needs to be held firm and helped to trust, but not to be arbitrarily punished.

Now move on to the more serious faults and actions about

which you feel guilty. Apply the same principles of forgiveness and making amends to them. You can learn from your harmful acts so that you are less likely to cause pain to yourself and others in the future. See your guilt not as a ball and chain that enslaves you, but as a warning beacon that illuminates your whole being, including the destructive and selfish parts of you, and which can help you remain both true to yourself and loving towards others.

Transformation
'*From guilt to compassion; from self-loathing to self-acceptance.*'

SELF-PITY

'Self-love, my liege, is not so vile a sin as self-neglect.' (Henry V)

Self-pity is generally considered to be a 'bad' thing. Someone who is deeply depressed may berate themselves – 'It's only self-pity, just pull yourself together and get on with it'. This is surprising. After all, pity and sorrow are among the most touching and compassionate of emotions, so why should it be so disgraceful to feel pity or sorrow for oneself ?

> *pity and sorrow are among the most touching and compassionate of emotions*

The answer has something to do with the fact that what usually goes under the heading of 'self-pity' is nothing of the sort. Genuine self-pity – a tender appreciation of the pain and hurt one has experienced, a holding of oneself in nurturing and forgiving arms – is, in our puritanical culture, hard to achieve. Genuine self-forgiveness and self-acceptance lead on to a loving attitude to the world. But often self-pity is more like a covert reproach to the world for being so unfeeling or indifferent. It is saying, like Eeyore in *Winnie the Pooh*, 'Well since you all don't care about me, I'll jolly well have to care for myself '. Self-pity contains a subtle form of blame, aimed at making those near us feel uncomfortable. Implicit in it is the accusation 'It's all your fault, really'.

There is a passivity about self-pity, a repetitive quality that clings onto misery rather than really addressing the issues or trying to change things. Self-pity relies on the 'Yes, but…' strategy in which you complain endlessly and bitterly about your lot, but are terrified to consider the consequences of changing it. This is why someone stuck in a rut of self-pity generates such feelings of frustration in others.

Self-pity is the protest of the powerless. Children who are thwarted may retreat into self-pity, especially if they feel overwhelmed by the superior force of older siblings or insensitive parents. As adults we may resort to self-pity as a means of comforting ourselves when we feel unable to alter situations which are causing us pain.

> *Self-pity is the protest of the powerless*

Suggestions

As soon as we find the courage to make our feelings known openly and clearly, our self-pity evaporates. Our problems are still there, but we are now free to alter our attitude to them or remove ourselves from them. If you spend a lot of time complaining about your partner to everyone except him or her, and to your partner about everyone else, you are caught in the 'poor me' trap.

Mood-brood your self-pity in an accepting, not a critical, way. Reach out to the pain and hurt you are feeling. Suddenly you may realize 'Oh, I'm just feeling sorry for myself ', and become liberated and able to act. You can separate your anger from your longing for love and can decide which belongs where. Try to identify the legitimate anger in your self-pity. Who has in reality let you down or ignored your needs? Can you let them know how hurt you feel directly without resorting to the guilt-inducing tones of self-pity? Listen to your tone of voice as you complain. Is it whiny? Moaning? Implicitly reproachful? Are there notes of bitterness or envy in your self-pity? Do you see everyone else as much better off than you are ?

Inside your self-pity is a helpless, vulnerable part of you that longs to be focused on, for someone to make things all right again. Be kind to yourself. In your mind's eye hold yourself tight and feel the reassuring warmth that this brings. Self-nurture is not selfish. You need to move from self-pity to self-love. Are you really craving such soothing from someone near you? Can you ask them for it directly, even if they are also the 'cause' of some of your unhappiness? See your unhappiness as coming from within you, as a response to the way the world has treated you perhaps, but as something that is under your control which you can do something about. Using inner dialogue, change your habitual self-pitying, complaining style from, for example, 'He always goes off to the pub and leaves me to clear up…', to a direct statement such as 'I feel abandoned and neglected when you go off without me…'

Exercise: Counting your criticisms

Spend one whole day in which you refuse to complain about or criticize anyone or anything. Every time you notice a blaming or critical thought towards anyone, including yourself, note it down, but vow not to express it. As you write your list put it in the form of 'I' statements: 'I am exasperated, I feel belittled, overlooked, angry, frustrated, impatient…'.

If you can own up to your feelings you will be released from self-pity, and this will lead to the uncomfortable but liberating realization that, rather than being a perfect person driven crazy by other people's imperfections, you, like everyone else, are a struggling and suffering being.

Transformation
'Self-pity points me towards my genuine pain and legitimate anger. I have the courage to accept my pain, and to act on my anger.'

SHAME

'His cheek is his biographer.' (Emily Dickinson)

The face is the mirror of the soul. Most emotions can be 'read' from someone's facial expression. This is particularly true of shame: we are shame-faced, lose face. When we are ashamed we feel ourselves blushing. We have a sense of being caught out, or caught at it, doing something by which we feel disgraced. It is as though there is an internal 'Big Brother' watching our actions, accusing us of weakness, childishness, nakedness. We are caught red-handed by our own personal persecutor.

Shame can be a deeper and more threatening emotion than guilt. You are guilty for what you have done, ashamed of what you are. If you are caught red-handed, you may feel guilt about the harm you have done to those from whom you have stolen, but feel ashamed of being seen to be a thief. We more readily admit to our crimes than our shame.

Shame and secrecy go together. In some families certain topics cannot be mentioned: sex, father's drinking, the dishonour of an illegitimate child or a bankruptcy. Shame drives feelings underground where they cannot be dealt with, mourned, or even effectively punished. We may have been lectured about the evils of stealing or lying, left feeling ugly and bad about our minor misdemeanours. We may have been punished for our natural exploratory interests, made to feel shameful and indecent. Disapproval, both within and outside the family, is paramount. 'What will the neighbours say ?' is the stuff of which shame is made. We long for love and acceptance, with all our faults and vulnerability and weakness.

Shame makes us feel that there are parts of us which can never be revealed, and so cuts us off from complete intimacy. Shame is transcended in sexual love in which lovers delight in every aspect of one another's bodies, and where the blush of shame is changed into the flush of excitement.

Suggestions

To transform shame you need to develop openness, self-assertion and forgiveness. There is nothing that cannot be talked

> **To transform shame you need to develop openness, self-assertion and forgiveness**

about, at least within yourself: 'nothing human is alien to me'. You came into the world naked and unashamed. You had nothing to hide then. Even if you are stripped of everything, however 'bad' you feel, purity and innocence are still there inside you: 'Thou art the thing itself... man is no more but such a poor, bare, forked animal as thou art.' (*King Lear*).

Exercise: On sexual shame

In your imagination relive situations in which you have felt ashamed. Rewrite the scenario – make things happen as you would have liked them to. Imagine, perhaps, that your mother discovers you and your brother playing 'doctors'. She is horrified. Imagine yourself saying as an adult what you perhaps did not have words to express then: 'Look mum, this is fascinating, I never knew that boys were like this. Please give me more information as I'm really interested and excited. There is nothing disgusting about genitals. They are part of our wholeness and completeness. We can reproduce through them. We can express feelings of closeness and affection. You and dad must be sexually aware and active or we would not be here.'

Exercise: What do you really want ?

Imagine you have been caught shoplifting. You are respectable, are not poor and consider yourself honest. Yet you take something that is not yours. Maybe you have done this many times and got away with it. Perhaps it excites you. Once you have got the objects home, they may not seem of much value, or you may be unable to enjoy them, knowing how you came by them. You are caught. What will your family and friends think? How can you conceal your shame? Recreate the scenario. The person who catches you takes you to a private room. He takes your hands, looks into your eyes and says: 'Taking things is wrong, but you will be forgiven if you can discover what you really want. Let's find that out and give it to you. Whatever you most desire you can have, but think deeply before you reply. Think of King Croesus who wanted everything to turn to gold and suffered for it. Perhaps you were mistaken in thinking you wanted a camera or a suit or a piece of jewelry. Is what you really want love, admiration, respect and a sense of your own value ?'

This will help you to begin to forgive yourself for what seemed so shameful. Is it such a crime to be depressed? Is it really your fault? If you had jaundice or a broken leg would you be feeling ashamed and blaming yourself in the same way? Do the neighbours matter or mind as much as you imagine? They will probably take their lead from you. Your teenage daughter is pregnant, but unmarried. If you accept her, support her and help her all you can, your neighbours will get out their knitting patterns too! If you can be compassionate towards yourself it will strike a chord in others. You 'make a fool of yourself ' – you fall over in a puddle scattering your shopping all around you. Your behaviour will dictate that of people around you. If you feel humiliated and ashamed to be seen lying on the ground with mud all over your clothes, passers-by will turn away. If you can laugh and ask for

> *If you can be compassionate towards yourself it will strike a chord in others*

help you will be surrounded by willing helpers.

Tranformation
'Shame shows me that I have a right to exist, to be loved, to make mistakes, to forgive myself and be forgiven.'

The spectrum of depression

Imagine these statements as opposite poles; see where you put yourself – now, and after trying out some of the exercises in this book.

When I am depressed I :

1. a) Feel hopeless, a failure and out of touch with the positive side of my life.
   b) Can still count my blessings, however bad I feel. I am impressed by the depth and strength of my feelings.

2. a) Can't imagine that things will ever change or improve.
   b) Know that these feeling will pass.

3. a) Am aggressive and standoffish to others – 'It's all their fault anyway'.
   b) Take responsibility for my feelings and am able to state 'I feel a bit gloomy' without making them feel guilty.

4. a) Don't look forward to or enjoy anything.
   b) Think of something I can do to help or please others.

5. a) Make pessimistic remarks about the state of the world, the government, teenagers, etc.
   b) Always try to lighten gloom and to see the funny side of things.

CHAPTER 7
THE YELLOW MOODS

ANXIETY

'Were the diver to think of the jaws of the shark he would never lay hands on the pearl.' (Sa'di)

Our body tells us when we are anxious. A hollow feeling in the pit of the stomach, a pounding heart, a tight chest, shallow rapid breathing, tension and an inability to keep still, sweating, knees like jelly, feeling faint – who has not experienced these at some time or other? It is all very well when we know the cause: the race about to be run, the examination about to start, the interview we are waiting for, the doctor's appointment. But often there is no obvious reason, and when that happens the symptoms of anxiety may themselves become a source of anxiety. 'If my heart goes on racing like this, I am bound to have a heart attack. Probably there is something wrong with my heart anyway – otherwise why should it beat so ferociously. That dizzy feeling must be coming from the brain – I just know I've got a brain tumour. I can't walk properly, probably I'm developing multiple sclerosis or some other horrible wasting disease.'

Now it is not just your body but your mind that has gone haywire. Your thoughts go into overdrive, imagining all the awful things that could possibly happen. If you are waiting for someone to come home and they are delayed, in your mind they have been killed in a car crash, mugged or raped – or perhaps they are having an affair, obviously they are tired of you and you are about to be ditched or divorced. If you make a mistake at work – you are bound to be found out and sacked on the spot. Your thoughts go round and round in circles –

now you begin to worry that you are going mad.

For some, anxiety seems to pervade every aspect of life – this is 'free-floating anxiety'. Others are bothered by specific fears – of heights, dogs, spiders, aeroplanes, crowds. These are easier to manage in one way, by avoiding the object of anxiety – but at a cost, since this inevitably means that life becomes restricted. Often we refuse things, an invitation to a party for instance, without really knowing why we said 'no', and when we start to think about our behaviour, more often than not fear and anxiety lie behind our avoidance.

EXAMPLE: GULLIVER'S NON-TRAVELS

For Susan almost every aspect of life was beset with fear. A married woman in her twenties with two children, she worried constantly about their health and that of her family. If they looked a little pale, they must have leukaemia. If they forgot to say goodbye when going to school, that was a bad omen – something bad was bound to happen that day. If her husband was five minutes late from work, it was certain that he had had a terrible car accident. Even if her children were happy, that was an ominous sign because happiness cannot possibly last. Leaving the house was a nightmare for her – the further from home she was, the less safe she felt. Travel was impossible – motorways hell on earth, and aeroplanes could not even be mentioned. Much of her day was spent in performing ritual acts – counting the corners of the room, turning round three times, aligning the furniture in the living room – which she hoped would magically avert disaster. All this had to be concealed, if possible, from herself ('I try not to think about it') and at all costs from her family, to whom she always presented a happy smiling face. As a child she was convinced that her parents far preferred her younger brother and would only like her if she was 'good' and happy. She described herself as 'totally stuck – tied down like Gulliver by thousands of tiny daily fears'. Listing, and so becoming aware of the extent of, her fears was at first very threatening to her, but to her surprise she also began to have brief spells when she felt free of them. She could hardly believe it was possible. 'It's as though I've taken a happiness drug,' she said.

Anxiety can be understood in terms of attachment. Throughout our lives we are bonded to a small number of people to whom we turn in times of trouble: parents,

> *Anxiety can be understood in terms of attachment*

brothers and sisters, spouses, children, intimate friends. If we feel threatened, we seek out our attachment figures who we know will protect us and with whom we feel safe. If they are not there, or cannot respond to our anxiety, it will get worse rather than being assuaged. A child who is hurt or frightened or tired will cling to his parent until the pain or the threat or the exhaustion has passed.

As we grow up the same process goes on inside us: we develop an 'internal parent' to whom we turn in times of trouble, whose metaphorical hand we hold at times of stress or threat. This may also take the form of religion, or an idea ('nothing venture, nothing gain'; 'faint heart never won fair lady'), or a comforting image. There will always be times when we need someone to turn to, to share our experience. Soldiers in battle stick together; we take a relation or friend with us when we go to the doctor; we like to be seen off when we set out on a journey (or if we don't, it is because that is how we avoid the anxiety and sadness of parting). But where attachments have been and are insecure – if a parent is unresponsive to our fears or absent altogether – then anxiety, rather than being allayed, grows. We have not had the vital experience of facing our fears with the help of a supportive parent or companion, and so we resort to avoidance. Lacking our own strong internal parent (see p. 24), we cling to those around us for security and dread being separated from them. The ultimate threat is the threat of death, of being separated from life itself.

Suggestions

Acute anxiety requires emergency measures. That is why relaxation and breathing exercises are so important. The more you have practised them in tranquillity, the easier it is going to be for you to cope when you have a bad attack of anxiety. If you are feeling suddenly overwhelmed with fear, wherever you are, whatever you are doing, try to relax each part of your body and steady your breathing. Controlling the breath will help to calm your agitated mind. Try to focus your thoughts on the present moment: the chair you are sitting on, your own hand, some flowers in a vase. Just look at them intently and deeply and try to eliminate all thoughts of the past or future from your mind. Think to yourself: 'Feelings of anxiety are arising in me. These feelings are so familiar to me that I can smile or even laugh at them'. Watch the thoughts from the safe haven of your untroubled self.

Try imagining that your worst fears have taken place. Perhaps you visualize the death of someone you love. Picture the event in as much detail as you can. See yourself coping with this and planning the practical things that need to be done. See how strong and calm you remain. Remind yourself that you have the ability to change your state of mind, however much external events are beyond your control.

Sometimes you fail to recognize anxiety for what it is. If it leads you to think you are physically ill, you may need to spend a lot of time tracking your anxiety down. Use your mood diary and try to develop as comprehensive a picture as you can of all the physical and emotional effects anxiety has on you and your behaviour. Take your fears seriously. Anxiety is too often dismissed as 'irrational' or childish. Try, as you would with a frightened child, to accept your anxiety, give yourself permission to feel it. Say to yourself: 'I have a right to feel anxious'. After all aeroplanes do crash sometimes, and usually without survivors; people do die from heart attacks; and, in South America at least, spiders can be poisonous. This does not mean, however, that you have to go along with all your fears. Calculate what the chances are that this particular plane might crash in view of the thousands of flights that take off daily without mishap; find out how many fit men or women of your age and weight do actually die from heart attacks; discover the number of people who have died from spider bites in the U.K. in the past ten years. That might reassure you a little, and you can use your mood chart to plot the level of your anxiety.

When your anxious thoughts seem to spiral out of control, don't try to stop them – that is like trying to control a runaway horse, the more frightened you are the more

Take an interest in your anxiety without trying to suppress or condone it

he will sense it and the faster he will bolt. Try to go with your thoughts, following them, observing them, riding, as it were, beside them. Take an interest in your anxiety without trying to suppress or condone it. You will find that this may stop the panicky thoughts, and at least you will not feel so out of control.

Welcome your anxiety as a mark of your awareness and sensitivity towards the world, and as a spur to action. True bravery comes from mastering fear, not from foolhardy or mindless recklessness. If you manage to do something that scares you – walking along a precipitous path in the mountains or, if you are agoraphobic, going shopping on your own – praise yourself and see it for the magnificent achievement that it is. Say to yourself: 'I am a warrior, not a worrier'. Think of the strong part of yourself that can lead the frightened child-part by the hand. Picture your strength as a rock, a mountain, or visualize yourself as the captain of a ship who remains calm while the sea is storm-tossed, and everyone else is in panic. Trust yourself and the universe. Look at your hand: see how it resembles your mother's or father's hand which you held as a child, there to protect you. Stroke your brow with your hand: your mother or father is stroking you and soothing you. There is nothing to be ashamed of. Like everyone, you want, need and deserve protection and security.

Since so many roads of anxiety lead ultimately to death, it is very helpful if you can reconsider your attitude towards death. Unless you believe in hellfire, death can be seen as the ultimate relief from suffering, a necessary part of life: 'If it be now, 'tis not to come; if it be not to come, it will be now; if it be not now, yet it will come: the readiness is all.' (Hamlet).

Make friends with death: picture the calm, the peace, the flowers that spring up from a grave. See death not as an ending but as a transformation, a change of state in which the atoms and energy which make up your body are transformed into something different, but never cease to exist. Compare a human life with the cycles of nature in which a cloud 'dies' as it becomes rain, which itself 'dies' as it becomes a river, which in turn 'dies' as it flows into the sea and evaporates to form a cloud once more. Think of your family and friends – you will live on in their memories, just as your lost loved ones live on in you. The more you feel able to accept death, the more you will value and enter deeply into life and the stronger you will feel in your fight against fear.

Anchor yourself in the present moment. Anxiety is based on thoughts of the precariousness and unpredictability of life – balance these with an appreciation of the huge power of the life-force within us, a product of millions of years of evolution, ensuring our survival and giving us strength to overcome danger. Many anxious people, when faced with a real crisis or life-threatening situation are amazed to find within themselves a calmness and capacity to cope they did not know they had.

Transformation
'From anxiety to an appreciation of the strength of the life-force and the unending cycles of nature.'

FEAR

'The wise man in the storm prays not for safety from danger but for deliverance from fear.' (Emerson)

Fear is perhaps the most primitive of the 'bad' moods, and with the other 'pure' emotional states – sorrow and anger – underlies almost all of them. When we suffer extreme pain or fear the brain becomes overwhelmed with sensation and we lose our usual intellectual analyser and interpreter. We just are: we become our fear or pain. When our life is suddenly in danger – the house is on fire, the car skids out of control, we are caught in a strong current and cannot swim back to the shore – we respond instinctively. There is no time to think. We act, and afterwards may feel a sense of awe at the superhuman strength we found within, enabling us to save ourselves and others from peril. Pure fear has led to an automatic survival response of flight or fight. We only feel the fear, the trembling and the shock after the event.

Terror in a controlled form is attractive to many people who seek it, either directly or vicariously, through such outlets as car racing, mountaineering, fairground rides or watching horror movies. The arousal associated with danger can have an exhilarating quality, and the satisfaction and relief of fear mastered increases self-esteem and self-confidence.

> *arousal associated with danger can have an exhilerating quality*

The capacity to cope with fear is central to a sense of well-being. Fear reminds us of the balance we need to strike between exploration and self-protection. If we can master our fears we are free to explore the world, but if we ignore them altogether we are likely to run into danger. For the fearful the world is a place populated with wild beasts, full of dangerous precipices and bottomless pits. To overcome fear we have to learn to tame the wild beasts, make the rough places smooth, plumb the depths.

Suggestions

There are many useful methods for overcoming fears – don't be frightened of fear! The first is the 'ladder' method. Make a list of all your fears. Then arrange them in order from lesser to greater. Put your foot on the lowest rung of the fear 'ladder': start with the least frightening. Once you have learned to say 'boo' to a gosling you will soon find yourself saying it to the biggest goose.

Exercise: Fear of flying

In your efforts to overcome fear, the reassurance and mastery that comes from breathing can be a great help. If you can control your breath you can cope with anything – you will overcome your irrational fears and keep a cool enough head when faced with real danger. Let us say you are terrified of flying and are due soon to go on an aeroplane. As departure looms you feel increasingly fearful. Practise your breathing and relaxation every day. Begin to

---

picture the plane as vividly as you can in your mind. Examine every part of it, the cabin, the engines, the wings; introduce yourself to the pilot. As you do so, continue to breathe and relax. Stay safely breathing in the present moment and don't allow your mind to wander to future possibilities. When you board the plane repeat the exercise, and return to it at the time of landing and whenever symptoms of anxiety arise.

When we are frightened we want more than anything the reassurance of someone who is not afraid. Become your own friend. There is an unafraid part of yourself that is always with you and willing to reassure you, if you can listen and escape from the force of the panic within you. Summon up the image of your inner friend or the image of a real person to help you through your difficulty.

EXAMPLE: NOT ALONE AFTER DEATH

Mary and Bill had worked hard bringing up their children and looked forward to the time when the children would leave home and they could be together and do all the things they had not had time or money to do before. When Bill died suddenly of a heart attack while playing squash, Mary felt shaken to the core and terrified of being on her own. Her fears got worse when, soon after the funeral, her house was burgled. Her terrors were worst at night. She told herself that her husband would have wanted her to be brave, and summoned up his spirit to help her cope. Every morning when she had got through another night she would turn to the chair where he used to sit and ask him 'Did I do all right ?', and visualized his response: 'You did very well – I'm proud of you'.

Use your powers of imagination and sense of humour to outwit the paralysing effects of fear.

Exercise: Terrified of parties

Let us say you are afraid of meeting new people, especially at parties. Your first instinct is to refuse the invitation, or, if you just can't get out of it, to cling on to the one person you know there and ignore the others. Escape from your passivity into an active role. Make it your task to find the people who feel lonely, left out, or know no one. Go up to them and talk to them. You might imagine you have been sent by your local paper to cover the event. As a reporter you will want to find out what the guests do, and where they come from. Like all good reporters you will set them at their ease by telling them your name, asking them theirs, and starting the conversation with innocuous and unthreatening questions such as whether they live nearby.

Before you know what has happened you will find that, with your courageous self in charge, your anxieties have diminished and you may even begin to enjoy yourself. As you overcome these smaller fears you will regain faith in your ability to take risks and survive.

Although most fears are imaginary, there may be moments in our lives when our worst fears are realized – the death of a child, a life-threatening illness, a house burned down. When faced with these dramatic and powerful experiences we may be surprised to find within us enormous powers and strengths we could not have believed we possessed. 'Present fears are less than horrible imaginings' (*Macbeth*): a successfully negotiated trauma can make you fearless in the face of the mind's 'horrible imaginings'.

Transformation
'*In my pure terror I discover the spontaneity of my drive towards self-preservation.*'

LONELINESS

'All man's unhappiness derives from one source – not being able to sit quietly in a room.' (Pascal)

Loneliness is an extreme form of disconnectedness. We do not have to be alone to feel lonely – we could be lying in

> *Loneliness is an extreme form of disconnectedness*

bed beside our partner or at a family gathering and still feel a deep sense of alienation and separation. Conversely, it is quite possible to 'wander lonely as a cloud' and feel at peace – at one with nature and the whole universe – even if we haven't spoken to anyone for days. This latter state is best referred to as solitude, as opposed to the pain of loneliness which, as one woman said, 'rises like a cold tide, deeply, oceanically sad', chilling our heart and filling us with fear and feelings of vulnerability and reminding us of our transience and insignificance. When we are lonely the whole world seems cold and unyielding, indifferent to our existence. We can see other people, plants and animals, but as though through ice impenetrable to our feeble attempts to make contact with life.

Loneliness and loss go together. If you are newly divorced or bereaved, the whole world seems to consist of united couples and families, laughing together, going home together, going on holiday together. Together. Always together. You ache with a sense of emptiness. 'Do I exist at all ?' you ask yourself as the happy couples look straight through you.

In a state of loneliness you may grasp at anyone who comes your way, eager to extinguish the pain of isolation. But your heart remains frozen: a brief moment of glancing intimacy perhaps and you are alone once more. Your estrangement from the world may feel like an agony of rejection, but from the outside you may seem aloof, apart, indifferent, snooty, superior. You have banished yourself from the world so as to make sure you will never be rejected again. You reason that self-imposed exile is better than banishment by forces over which you have no control.

In contrast, solitude is a necessary balm, a coming home to the self that is needed at times of stress or overstimulation. Like Greta Garbo we all want to be alone sometimes – to recover our equilibrium, to recall private moments of happiness, when we read a letter from a lover, or struggle with the exultation or disappointment that only we can face when we open our exam results. Bread needs to be left undisturbed if the yeast is to make it rise. We need to withdraw into a temporary private cell if changes in our lives are to be digested and allowed to have their full effects.

Suggestions

Realizing the distinction between loneliness and being alone is vital. Rushing out and joining clubs can simply reinforce your sense of isolation. Get in touch with your loneliness. You feel deeply separate and unloved. You find it impossible to believe or remember that your parents, friends, brothers and sisters care or ever have cared about you. Give yourself permission not to be terrified of your aloneness. 'Hello loneliness – you are back again are you? Make yourself at home, feel free, I'm not afraid of you. You try to tell me that we are born and die alone, but that is not true, because I have my inner resources to keep me company.'

> **Exercise: On connectedness**
>
> Now come back to your breath. As you breathe, feel the air as it passes your nostrils keeping you alive. Breathing connects us with the universe. Picture the cycle of nature in which the plants and trees need the carbon dioxide you exhale to convert the sun's energy into chlorophyll and offer in exchange the fresh oxygen which you breathe into your lungs. Visualize how life is sustained by this rim of atmosphere which clings to it like mist on a hillside on an autumn morning.
>
> You feel frozen, congealed. Imagine you are a daffodil bulb in winter, lying dormant, waiting patiently for the warmth of spring to come when you will burst forth into flower. The bulb has to endure many months of solitude beneath the cold earth. See yourself as an unhatched chick growing, developing, changing beneath the smooth surface of an apparently unaltering eggshell – protected, but vulnerable if exposed too soon.

Like the mother hen you have to brood your loneliness, trusting that one day the ice in your heart will melt, freeing you at last to reach out and rediscover the world and your place in it. Think of yourself as a good, unobtrusive mother who is there for her child playing happily by herself, secure in the knowledge that she is watched over by a silent loving presence. That child – who only hours earlier may have been terrified by a nightmare in which she was being preyed on by a wild beast – is now learning the delights of solitude.

Eventually you will want to make contact with other people. You will find, almost by accident, that you have something in common with others. As you walk your dog, or chat in a shop, or drop your professional facade at work for a moment, you will suddenly find a connection has been made, perhaps even on the basis of a shared dislike. Crises and common causes, whether national or local, often bring people together and you may find yourself swept up in a campaign which you would never have dreamed of having anything to do with.

At some point you will feel brave enough to speak aloud about your loneliness – perhaps even to the point where you can ring someone up and suggest a meeting: 'I've been feeling really cut off lately – I'd love to do something with you sometime'.

As your loneliness dissolves you will begin to enjoy your solitude more and more. You are free to do as you please, unconstrained by having to adapt to the needs of others. You can arrange your days as you like, making routine tasks into pleasurable and meaningful events which put you in touch with yourself and everything around you. Wash yourself with care and love, think about the food which you eat, appreciate radio and television and the powers of communication that man has devised! You will be sensitive to your pets and your garden and to the world of nature of which you are a part. Strengthened in your capacity to be alone, you will have mastered one of the hardest hurdles we have to overcome.

Transformation
'From the pain and fear of loneliness to the pleasures of solitude.'

OUT OF CONTROL

'Where life becomes a spasm
And History a whiz
If that is not sensation'
I don't know what it is.' (Lewis Carroll)

Your heart races, your mind is in overdrive, you rush from one thing to another with enormous energy. You seem to accomplish great things in no time at all. But in this state of excitement, initially so attractive and envy-making, all may not really be well. You buy things extravagantly, impulsively, in super-abundance. Clothes seem irresistible, foreign travel a must; there has to be endless activity, movement, events happenings. No sooner have you arrived somewhere than you are thinking about where you are going to next. Your new car is already out of date, you must trade it in for another. Your partner is dull and boring – why not get rid of him and find someone better? Endlessly searching you are never at peace, quiet in yourself, centred or balanced.

EXAMPLE: MOTHER HUBBARD AND HER SHOES

Enid, who was in her seventies and living on a small pension, went on a year-long shopping spree after her husband died. When she herself became ill and had to go into hospital three years later, her children found over 100 pairs of shoes in her wardrobe, many never worn.

It is as though you are on an express train dashing through the countryside so fast that you only get a fleeting impression of it. The destination is irrelevant, the important thing is to stay on the move. Your way of life may look exciting from the outside, but actually being in such a manic state is not much fun after a while. All your pleasure is in anticipation. Your need is insatiable. Nothing satisfies or nourishes you. You are driven by some inner force that is not under your control.

Underlying your 'high' and whirlwind state of mind there is fear: fear that if you were to stop for a moment you might be hit by depression, a painful realization of the chaos in your life and of the unhappiness you are causing to yourself and others. The widow with the 100 pairs of shoes could not face the loneliness and sorrow of her bereavement. Behind the party-going and the rushing about and the drinking and the opportunistic sex there may be a hollow feeling of purposelessness that has to be staved off at all costs. You may doubt your capacity to engage with life or be valued as a person unless you are always in a flurry of excitement.

Sometimes being out of control goes in the opposite direction to the whirlwind that carries you 'high' above the everyday world. It is a whirlpool that threatens to suck you under with an overwhelming pressure of responsibilities and emotions you can't cope with. No sooner have you paid one bill than another appears. Your marriage is breaking down and you have got to take your child to hospital and the mortgage company is threatening to repossess the house and your mother is ill and you get cautioned about arriving late for work and the school rings about your other child playing truant and the car refuses to start in the morning and... and...

Suggestions

Find a still place inside yourself from which you can watch your speeding self. If you are 'high', don't try to stop rushing – admire your energy and brilliance, the swooping flights of your airborne self. Then imagine yourself as a kite on a string,

> *Find a still place inside yourself from which you can watch your speeding self*

gradually being pulled towards earth, feeling heavier and heavier as you near the ground. See your manic self as also fearbound, terrified of misery and loneliness. In your mind's eye hold yourself tight so that you cannot fly off again. Say calming things to yourself: 'It is all right... I am strong... resilient... I can survive...'.

Subtle methods are needed to cope with being out of control. The more you try to put on the brakes, the more frustrated and desperate you may become. Like a skilful judo player, you have to go with the forces that are making you fall, but turn them to your advantage. Moods, like fairground rides, have a course to run, but sooner or later they come to a stop. A big fish on a fragile line can be played until it is exhausted enough to be landed. John Gilpin's horse (William Cowper, the author of the famous poem, suffered from manic-depression) eventually reached exhaustion point.

Fighting the feeling of being out of control often makes it worse. Trust that things will come all right in the end. Sit very still and 'watch' your thoughts and feelings racing by. Detach yourself from them, but do not suppress them. Think to yourself: 'feelings of loss of control are arising in me'.

When the feeling of being out of control threatens, breathe steadily to slow yourself down. Focus on the present moment, the richness of now. The storm is raging, but it will not last for ever. Enjoy the power of the waves as they lift you up – a tiny vessel in an ocean of energy. Trust your own buoyancy. If you panic you will feel yourself sinking. If you trust the sea you will find, as in a dream, that you can survive beneath the waves and marvel at the depths and caverns that lie within you. Sooner or later you will come to the surface – in the warm waters of a calm glassy sea where you can swim to a sunlit beach where you can lie quiet and still.

Transformation

'From feeling out of control to a recognition of the power of the tremendous forces that are within me. From fear of madness to trusting the universe.'

The spectrum of anxiety

Where do you stand on the spectrum of anxiety ?

When I feel anxious I :

1 a) Always assume the worst.
   b) Acknowledge my anxiety and know that it can't
   affect the outcome.

2 a) Feel tense, shaky, short of breath and faint.
   b) Take control of my breathing and make a
   conscious effort to relax.

3 a) Feel all alone with my fears.
   b) Share my worries with trustworthy others.

4 a) Mistrust those on whom I have to depend –
   doctors, dentists, solicitors, teachers, pilots.
   b) Recognize the irrational component of my fears,
   own them and don't blame them on other people.

5 a) Am paralysed with fear.
   b) Imagine my worst fears happening and myself
   coping.

CHAPTER 8
THE RED MOODS

ANGER

'To be angry with the right person to the right extent and at the right time and with the right object and in the right way – that is not easy.' (Aristotle)

The earliest physical manifestations of anger are very similar to those that go with fear: an uneasy sensation in the centre of the body around the stomach, chest and throat; a prickling at the back of the neck; awareness of your heart thumping. Anger, like fear, often arises in response to threat, hurt or rejection. But when we are angry we deal with threat by fight, not flight. When we are afraid, angry feelings are suppressed and we try to remove ourselves from the situation. When we are angry, our feelings erupt, surging up within us like a volcano, filling and flushing us with red-hot ire, as we try to impose ourselves on a situation by which we feel threatened.

Those who can control and direct their anger appropriately are fortunate. They stand their ground when they need to. They can clear the air if they feel misunderstood or neglected by their loved ones. They do not bow to the majority if they feel it is wrong to do so. They will fight injustice when necessary. They can reprimand their children without terrorizing or belittling them. They are not afraid to show their

Those who can control and direct their anger appropriately are fortunate

strength, but avoid bullying. They are not craven or cowardly, nor are they belligerent or destructive. They exemplify the healthy aspects of anger – its cleansing and clearing powers, its assertion of selfhood, its power to make a firm boundary, to stake a territory in rough or uncertain ground.

For many of us, however, anger is not that simple. Typically, people have difficulty either in controlling anger or in expressing it. For some, anger threatens to spill out at the slightest provocation. Someone 'cuts you up' while driving – you hurl abuse at them at the next traffic light. The children leave the living room in a mess – you scream and shout at them while they cower dejectedly. Your partner forgets to buy something you asked for and you rant and rave about it. Accusations follow as you climb the escalator of mutual anger, and a full scale row breaks out in which both of you say things you don't really mean.

In contrast to this 'hair-trigger' anger there are those who just cannot get hold of their anger at all. Chronic unexpressed anger is a corroding and deadening force which underlies many unhappy moods: depression, apathy, boredom. It may manifest itself in physical symptoms or illness – chronic back pain or emotion-triggered asthma. Anger unexpressed can make you feel like an automaton, going through your daily routines like a robot, frightened to express any feelings for fear of the explosion of rage which might happen if you did. Many people base their lives and their security around pleasing and looking after others. For them suddenly to release the years of resentment and disappointment which they have accumulated seems like an impossible and dangerous task. They have dealt with the threat of rejection by submission rather than healthy protest. If the worm of compliance finally turns, the results can be dramatic.

EXAMPLE: ANGER ACCEPTED

Peggy, a painter in her fifties, twice divorced, finally felt she had found the right man for her. She behaved as she had done in most of the other relationships in her life by trying to please and ingratiate herself with him while concealing her true feelings. To her dismay he was unmoved by these attempts, although he showed her respect and genuine fondness. She began to feel more and more confused by this relationship from which she had expected so much. She began to feel furious with her boyfriend for his apparent unresponsiveness. Layer upon layer of buried anger stirred within her. She saw him as heartless and self-centred, like the parents whom she had tried so desperately and so unsuccessfully to please as a child. She stayed up all night writing all this down in a letter which she presented to him at breakfast and, trembling and tearful with rage and fear, read out to him. Her greatest fear – and it was this that had held back the anger for all those years – was that her rage would be found unacceptable and that he would retaliate by walking out. To her amazement he listened thoughtfully, agreeing with the points he thought valid, but strongly resisting the equation between himself and her parents. Following this their relationship was much stronger and deeper.

Anger is a double-edged weapon. It can be a vital part of self-assertion and self-defence, and failure to express anger can

We need to listen carefully to our anger since it can tell us what we really want

lead to chronic low self-esteem and misery. But anger can also be immensely destructive, killing the very love and security which it seeks. Being angry with your loved ones forces them to take notice of your feelings, but also runs the risk of driving them away or making them retaliate, thus crushing your feelings even more. We need to listen carefully to our anger since it can tell us what we really want. At the same time we need to be able to curb its tendency to get out of control and so destroy what we love most dearly.

Suggestions

The aim is to transform the externally destructive effects of 'hair-trigger' anger, and the internally destructive effects of suppressed anger, into positive self-assertion and disclosure of feelings.

The first step, as always, is to observe anger as it arises: 'Hello anger – here you are at last' or ' I'm strong enough to contain you and put you to good use'. Breathe deeply so as to be aware of your anger, neither suppressing nor becoming overwhelmed by it.

Exercise: Recording your rage

For 'hair-trigger' anger a mood diary can be very useful. Keep a record of your outbursts of rage and feelings of fury and try to write down what the circumstances were that provoked them. When and why and with whom were you angry? Does a pattern begin to emerge? Do your outbursts usually happen when you are tired, hungry or have had a drink? Are they always directed at one particular person? Are you really angry about something quite different, but blaming that person because they happen to be nearby or are weaker than you ?

EXAMPLE: THE BAD OLD DAYS

For much of Tom's childhood, his father, a miner, had been unemployed. Tom had been determined to escape from poverty and had built up a very successful building firm. His children went to private schools some miles away from the comfortable suburb where he lived. He found himself feeling furious and shouting at the children every morning as they never seemed ready for him to drive them to school in good time. Then he began to realize that his resentment dated back to the time when he was a child. His mother, preoccupied with his younger sisters, had expected him to walk to school on his own, and took little interest in what happened to him while he was there. The pattern was repeating itself, as he now felt that his children's needs took precedence over his. His anger was fuelled by his envy of the comfort and concern which his children had in abundance (thanks, he thought, to his hard work and sacrifice) but which he had felt so lacking in his own childhood.

Looking deeply into our anger in this way can help us to find feelings of pain and rejection in ourselves to which we have been blind, and alert us to the unhappiness of those towards whom we direct our anger.

EXAMPLE: AN OFFICE CONFLICT

Ben, a local government officer in his thirties, was in constant conflict with a woman colleague in his office. Every time she spoke he felt irritated, and he was constantly aware of her inefficiency, laziness and greedy attitude towards office 'perks'. On looking into his anger he began to see that what really annoyed him was her close friendship with a rival in the office and obvious admiration for his talents. He began to see the envy which lay behind his anger, and to recognize his own greed, which he was at such pains to hide, in the light of this woman's more blatant egotism. Having looked into his own reactions he could see hers more clearly, and understand her behaviour as an expression of her own lack of confidence, and her need to stoke the fires of conflict as a legacy of past neglect. Once he had grasped some of this, it became much easier for him to express his justified anger about her poor time-keeping without it flaring up into a destructive conflagration.

be less afraid of your anger

Unexpressed anger needs to be released from its confinement, brought out into the light. To do this you need to be less afraid of your anger, to value it and greet it as long-lost friend. Think of it as a child who needs to have a tantrum from time to time, whose parents will calmly allow it to scream and shout and stamp its foot, firmly making sure that things don't get out of control and trying all the while to listen attentively and get to the root of what is upsetting the child.

EXAMPLE: SECRET WEAPONRY

Julie, a very efficient secretary in her mid-forties, worked for a car-hire firm. She was well liked by all her customers and by the bosses of the firm. Most of the people she had dealings with were male and they both patronized and relied on her. She never openly expressed resentment, but when she got home in the evening, she would pour herself a drink and then mentally line up everyone who had annoyed her in the course of the day and shoot them! The size of the gun was matched to the gravity of the offence caused: small irritations were punished with a pistol, larger ones with an automatic rifle, and real humdingers were responded to with bazookas!

Exercise: Cushion-bashing

Sometimes it can help to hit a cushion with your hand, starting quietly, saying 'I hate you...' over and over again, building up to a crescendo. It is often good to have a friend to help you with this, since it may bring up all kinds of different feelings as well as the hatred or rage which you started with. You may become tearful, frightened, and feel vulnerable and exposed.

Exercise: Writing a letter to someone with whom you feel angry

Writing a letter to someone with whom you feel angry can be a useful way of getting in touch with buried feelings. Try to pour your heart out into the letter, don't hold back. After you have written the letter, put it aside and re-read it after a day or two. You will probably find you now don't want or need to send the letter. You may want to keep it as a reminder to yourself of how you felt. Alternatively you may create a ritual in which you burn the letter, imagining all your hatred and fury turning to ash and going up in smoke along with the paper.

These exercises help you gather your anger into a usable form. Sooner or later you will want to confront in reality, not phantasy,

gather your anger into a usable form

whoever or whatever it is that has made you angry. Rehearse what you want to say: 'There is something I want to discuss with you. I am very angry because of what you did and said...'.

Realize that anger, like mourning, has a course to run and, if expressed, will often lead to reconciliation and change.

Transformation

'Expressing my feelings openly keeps me emotionally healthy. The more honestly I can express my feelings, the more I will be able to love and be loved.'

BITTERNESS

'Sour grapes can never make sweet wine.' (Thomas Fuller)

Only something which was expected to be sweet can turn to bitterness. Bitterness is the last dregs of hope and optimism, the hunger and thirst of dashed hopes.

Our envy leaves an enduring sense of bitterness

Life has let us down. We have invested our emotions and energies, many years of nurture and concern, in a child, a project, a business, only to have our cherished dream snatched from us. Our child may die, our projects fail, our business dissolve. We gave our all – commitment, love, unceasing work – for nothing.

What we most desire does not reach fruition. We feel a hopeless victim of ill fate or malice. As these external disappointments accumulate (they may not be as dramatic as the ones we have depicted, just an endless string of everyday rejections and failures), so our internal world becomes increasingly barren. Our inner seedlings wither and die. We have been just as attentive as our neighbour or more so – yet their crop flourishes while ours comes to nothing. Our envy leaves an enduring sense of bitterness. We are swamped by feelings of the unfairness of things.

EXAMPLE: THE UNFAIRNESS OF INFERTILITY

> Jill was infertile. She longed for a baby and had endured
> endless investigations and attempts at artificial insemina-
> tion, but to no avail. She felt unfulfilled, inadequate and
> bitter. Seeing mothers and children in supermarkets was
> extremely painful for her and when she heard that her
> ever-fecund neighbour was pregnant for the fourth time
> she fainted. Later she confessed how she longed for some
> harm to come to both woman and child. But admitting
> to these feelings seemed to produce a change. She
> abandoned her visits to the infertility clinic, and success-
> fully adopted twins!

Gradually the bitterness comes to pervade our whole being –
it begins to feel like us – we come to depend on it. It makes
sense of the injustice of the world and of our persistent feelings of misery and loneliness. We almost come to enjoy the
bitter taste of things, and the greater pain which we can
control blocks out the lesser over which we have no control,
or the absence of feeling altogether.

The embittered person can not allow her inner child to
prosper and thrive. Like the wicked fairy in *Sleeping Beauty*, the
uninvited guest at the christening feast can only hate and envy
the newborn baby – and wish her ill. The idea of self-nurture is
abhorrent and ridiculous: 'What good have kindness and love
ever done to anyone? What little I had was snatched away
from me, and I am tortured by the presence of love when it
comes near me, so certain am I that I will destroy it'.

Yet there can be a certain dignity, a coherence, a logic in
bitterness. Hopkins' lamentation – 'I am gall, I am wormwood'
– has the courage of a man crucified by doubt and depression
who is prepared, Christ-like, to face the pain and suffering of
life head on.

Suggestions

As a bitter person you are a mass of wounds which you will not allow to heal. Your bitter attitude invites further pain which serves to feed your bitterness even more. As you sit quietly, breathing, brooding on your bitterness, try to distil from it the pure pain and rejection which have so poisoned you. Allow yourself to feel the unadulterated feelings of loss and emptiness. Weep tears of anger or sadness. See how imperfection and separation are intrinsic parts of the processes of life. Like Dr Jekyll and Mr Hyde, there are two parts of you: one wants to attack your inner weakness and pain, to dash your pining infant to death. Acknowledge this feeling of revenge that cannot allow anything good to spring up within you for fear that it will be taken from you. Another part of you longs to bathe your wounds, to cleanse them, bandage them, give them a chance to heal. Imagine these two forces at work within you. You have the power to tip the scales in favour of reparation so that your wound can become a scar, not a living source of yet more bitterness. Take each of your hurts in turn and treat them like this. You will need to draw on your powers of forgiveness towards a world which seems to have dealt you such a cruel fate.

> *You have the power to tip the scales in favour of reparation so that your wound can become a scar, not a living source of yet more bitterness*

This is a hard task – but not impossible because you have within you many loving and generous impulses. Many people who are crippled by bitterness towards their fellow men and women have loving and loyal relationships with animals and plants. They agree with Madame Roland – 'The more I see of men, the better I like dogs!' Animals may seem preferable to humans – their love is unconditional and they do not retaliate, revenge themselves or abandon you. Your voice softens when you talk to your dog or cat. You can repay their devotion in kind. So too with gardens, where you may find the predictable fertility that so eludes you in the world of men. The well-tended plant grows tall and fine under your green fingers, and you will more easily forgive a late frost or a hungry snail that dashes your hopes, than you will a lover who lets you down or a boss who has no inkling of what it costs in effort and worry to keep him happy. When you draw on your love of the non-human world and find within you the seeds of healing, your bitterness will begin to turn to sweetness.

Transformation
'From bitterness to the sweet relief of forgiveness and new life.'

FRUSTRATION

'To lie in bed and sleep not. To wait for one who comes not. To try to please and please not.' (Egyptian proverb)

In frustration we are thwarted, baulked, snookered, stopped dead in our tracks. We are so near, and yet so far. We are over-whelmed with a feeling of utter exasperation and misery as we snatch defeat from the jaws of victory. Like Odysseus, we drift helplessly away from our promised land which is so tantaliz-ingly yet unreachably close, condemned to many more years of wandering. It may be a serious or a trivial desire, but we want it badly – a job, a boyfriend, a bus to arrive, the car to start in the morning, a sneeze to come, the builders to turn up. Whatever it is, it is not in our power to make it happen. The world refuses to dance to our tune.

In our frustration we look for something or someone to blame. We kick the car for failing to start, shout at the shop for being shut. We may even half forget what it was we really wanted – all we can feel is the frustration, the pent-upness, the mixture of anger and unhappiness. We remain in a state of suspense – 'If I just wait five more minutes he's bound to turn up' – imprisoned by our dependence on what seems an unreliable and indifferent world.

When we are frustrated our harmonious relationship with the world around us is disrupted. There is no give and take. We can accept the indifference of the universe if we know that our little corner of it will respond to our needs occasionally. If our inner state is balanced we can cope when the external world lets us down. But in frustration we expect all satisfactions to come from outside and when they fail we chafe furiously. We want something desperately that it is not within our power to get. We want to control the world rather than flow with it. We feel helpless as our attempts to dictate terms get us nowhere. We have lost our balance, our sense of humour and our realism.

Suggestions

People in a state of frustration are often told to calm down – good advice, although it may serve only to increase the feeling of frustration and annoyance if the one thing that would really do the trick just isn't available. But it is – breathing is your secret weapon against the inevitable frustrations of daily life. By focussing on your breathing you become calm: you are taken away from external events which you may be powerless to influence, and brought back to yourself.

> *become active rather than passive*

Once you have unhitched yourself from your yoke of frustration, you are better placed to appraise the situation. To free yourself you need to see through the black-and-white view of

the world that has dominated your thinking; you need to find
flexibility and give-and-take, to become active rather than
passive – sometimes going with what is offered, sometimes
refusing, always looking at things in a different light.

EXAMPLE: THE BROKEN WASHING MACHINE

Let us say your frustration is brought on by a broken washing machine. Think of all the opportunities this opens out.
You may be able to fix it yourself. Try unscrewing the back
– you may find that, as happened to one woman, a dead
mouse is shorting the electric circuit, and once it is
removed all is well! Your frustration has revealed self-help
skills you did not know you had. Or you can do the washing
by hand for once – by doing so mindfully you will become
aware of the millions of people who have no household
appliances, of the hundreds of years of human history
where washing was a weekly chore, of the skill and ingenu-
ity of the human hand and brain. Or you may decide to
leave things dirty for once – perhaps you are overconcerned
about cleanliness.

Perhaps your frustration is sexual. Mood-brooding on
your sexuality helps to put it into perspective. See beyond
your physical desire to the needy or neglected child
urgently demanding affection. Now try to look at things
from your partner's point of view. You begin to see him or
her not just as an object that inconveniently fails to meet
your need, but as a person with their own rhythms and
sensitivities. Rather than remaining passively stuck with
your frustration, talk to them about it, first in inner
dialogue, then in reality – they may be grateful to you for
having broached the subject. Sometimes all that is needed
is negotiation and mutual understanding for things to right

themselves. It may help if you can think of the funny side of the situation – it is rather comic when we see how often we are the plaything of our desires, and in any case laughter is one of the best aphrodisiacs!

Transformation

'I am no longer at the mercy of external events. With the help of my breathing, I choose how I react. I am actively in control of my life. The outside world supports me and offers many different possibilities.'

HATE

'I was angry with my friend
I told my wrath, my wrath did end.
I was angry with my foe :
I told it not, my wrath did grow.' (Blake)

Hate is like poison: when we see or think of someone we hate, we feel sick. There is an urgent need to rid ourselves of whatever seems hateful: our eyes

subordinated hatred makes us tense up, turn away, avert our gaze

look daggers; our heart is full of bile; we want to hurt, humiliate, annihilate the object of our hatred, to shout, spit or scream at them. Sometimes we hate everyone, the whole world. There is also a quieter, more defeated form of hatred which cannot be openly expressed – for example towards a teacher or boss or captor – in which we silently nurture our hatred and wish them every harm. This subordinated hatred makes us tense up, turn away, avert our gaze.

Hate can be an intense form of anger: more urgent and stronger. We hate those who threaten to remove from us the very thing we want most dearly. We fear the loss and want to annihilate the person who has it in their power to destroy us in this way: 'I hate and I love. I don't know why, but I feel it, and am in agony'. Catullus's verse strikes a chord in anyone who has been abandoned by someone they love, especially if they have been left for someone else.

Hate, like anger, can be healthy. The jilted lover needs to hang onto their hatred, at least for a while. A screaming baby or a furious adolescent is feeling his strength, but hoping that the hatred will be contained by stronger adults around them. There is a force in hatred: it can be like a cleansing fire which clarifies our most horrible feelings, and be a first step towards reconciliation. But chronic unexpressed hatred gnaws at us inside, corrupting our relationships, turning us sour and sulky. Hate craves – but fears – the light of recognition. Once exposed it often deflates and scuttles away into the darkness.

Suggestions

As with anger, the problem posed by hatred is to find a way of drawing on the power and self-assertion it contains rather than being poisoned by it. Reclaim your hate as part of you – detach it from the person to whom it is directed. Own it. Ask yourself: 'Is this hate helping me or holding me back ?' Think about the object of your hatred. Imagine them in your mind's eye. Walk round them, see them from all angles. Are there any features which remind you of yourself? Often we hate in others the very thing which we dislike about ourselves – we 'project' it into them where it can safely be attacked. They are 'hateful' – full of our own hate which, in our minds, we put into them. Try taking your own hateful feelings back into yourself. Accept that you are a mixture of good and bad feelings: your hatred is just one part of you. Can hatred turn into compassion? Can you separate out the hatred you feel for someone's actions, and still accept him as a person? Democracy is based on this idea – the British parliament is a good example of the co-existence of political hatred and personal cameraderie. Could confronting the person you feel so strongly about turn hatred into disagreement or reasoned objection? Hate hates reason, courage and humour. The Irish hostage Brian Keenan, who was brutally tortured while in solitary confinement in Lebanon for more than three years, found his hatred melting away when one day he heard his captor sobbing uncontrollably. He found a wave of intense pity for this hateful man sweeping over him.

Make a list of all the people and things you hate. Is there a pattern to them? Are they all women? Or people in authority? Or people who can't remember your name? Do they all make you feel inadequate or inferior? Try translating 'I hate X...' into 'My feelings of hatred are activated by...'. You may discover that it is a sense of powerlessness or helplessness or abandonment that arouses your feelings of hate.

Transformation
'I first own, and then release the feelings of hatred that are distorting my inner world and blocking me.'

IRRITABILITY

'Men often bear little grievances with less courage than they do large misfortunes.' (Αεσορ).

> **The sheer absurdity of this can, with luck, make us laugh**

We are irritable if the shoe pinches, when the door squeaks, at a dripping nose or leaking tap. When we are irritable we are picky and niggly, sometimes choosing absurd things to criticize or complain about: 'That shade of yellow really disgusts me'; 'You eat your cereal in a particularly provoking way'. Our being recoils from the world at these tiny points of contact. We know really that the problem lies within us, but we cannot help being provoked. In a state of premenstrual tension for example, when irritability is often at its height, it is quite common to feel revolted by anything – even a tree or a bird song. The sheer absurdity of this can, with luck, make us laugh and bring us back to how irritable we are feeling – to the realization that the problem is with ourselves, not it or them.

Being so petty and unjustifiably critical is mystifying. How can such strong feelings be aroused by a mere colour or tone of voice? The problem in irritability, as with the pinching shoe, is in the fit between us and the world. Feelings of irritation arise from unarticulated, undigested, unexpressed, confused emotions whose roots run much deeper. You are really saying: 'I don't feel loved, understood, part of the family'. You may need more attention than you are getting, or feel crowded in on and claustrophobic from too much intrusive attention. In a state of irritation the other person can never get it right. If you are ignored, you feel rejected: if they are attentive, you feel invaded.

Suggestions

Recognize your irritability and bring it back to yourself. The world is not out to drive you mad, it's the way you react to it. Is it PMT, or exhaustion, or suppressed anger? Your irritability with the way your husband clicks his jaw when he yawns, the way he clears his throat or cuts his toenails, may not be justified – but if he forgot all about your birthday, or hasn't had a proper conversation with you for days, then your irritability is a pointer to legitimate feelings which need to be expressed.

Irritability is most commonly an expression of neglect or being overstretched. You need to deal with your feelings for others, but in the end it comes back to the way you care for and love yourself. 'Sit' on your own needs. Breathe calmly and

> *Irritability is most commonly an expression of neglect or being overstretched*

evenly. Think of yourself as a fractious baby who needs absolute attention, calm, space and soothing. Cradle this baby in your arms. Feel the irritability melting away as your discomfort is gently massaged by loving hands. See the absurdity of your intense likes and dislikes. Think of yourself as an oyster secreting layer upon layer of mother-of-pearl until you have moved from feeling annoyed by the intruding grain of sand to gratitude to it for stimulating you towards self-soothing and creativity.

Transformation
'My irritability challenges me to care properly for myself, to attend to my inner world and to turn away from blaming and hitting out unnecessarily.'

RESENTMENT

'Let not the sun go down upon your wrath.'
(Epistle to the Ephesians)

Resentment is a grudging, low-grade mixture of anger and discontent. You are the underdog with the hang-dog look. You feel put upon, taken for granted, overlooked, unappreciated. Resentment smoulders, manifesting itself in the way you move about: you slam the door; you slap your husband's dinner down in front of him; you drag yourself up from your adolescent slump to do the task you feel has been unfairly imposed on you. 'It's really not fair', you feel. Everyone has a better deal than you – they are leading the life of Riley while you slave away. You live on a knife edge. If you say what you really think – show people how furious you feel – you run the risk of losing favour and position, albeit the second-rate one you are lumbered with. So you persist with the role you so despise yourself for tolerating. Meanwhile the slow corrosive fuse of resentment continues to burn inside you. Maybe one day the volcano of fury will finally erupt.

The boss promotes a younger, less experienced colleague; your mother-in-law compares your children unfavourably with her other grandchildren; your stepchildren help themselves to food from the fridge without asking, behaving as if you do not exist. All these fuel your resentment. You feel as if you are faced with an impossible choice. If you submit, you feel trampled on; if you complain, you run the risk of antagonizing people whose esteem you depend on. You bite back your rage. At worst you become a martyr, expecting or even embracing the downtrodden role.

As a child you may have felt similarly imposed upon. Perhaps you were the oldest child, who was expected to look after the younger ones while your mother produced more and more babies. Perhaps your mother was a single parent, and as the only male in the house you were expected to be a little 'husband' to her, looking after her and running errands for her. Perhaps your father expected you to help in his shop while all your friends were out playing. You still feel like that child now, unable to assert yourself or give yourself equal rights to other people. You swallow your feelings – but they come out in your posture and whiny tone of voice.

Suggestions

First recognize your resentment. Most of the time you may only be dimly aware that it is there. Try to catch it in the butterfly net of your awareness as it passes across your mind. Gently examine it. What is it that you really mind about? Is it a feeling that comes from a present injustice or does it belong to the past? Is it really the girl in the office who is always in the limelight that bothers you? Could

What is it that you really mind about?

this be a hangover from childhood where your sister seemed to get all the attention ?

EXAMPLE: TAKEN FOR GRANTED

Prue's parents had got on badly through much of her childhood. Her father, Raymond, a successful civil servant, was homosexual but had dutifully decided to wait until the children (Prue was the youngest of three) had left school before leaving his wife to live with a colleague with whom he had been having an affair for several years. Raymond felt deeply ashamed of his homosexuality, especially as he was an ardent Christian, and made no efforts to contact his children after the split-up, although he missed them greatly. Prue, a quiet self-effacing young woman, had always felt overlooked by her father whom she nevertheless admired. Then a curious thing happened. On her twenty-fifth birthday he sent her a substantial cheque – just what she needed for the deposit on a flat she was after. She felt a mixture of contradictory emotions: gratitude and relief at the money, but huge resentment about being ignored for so many years and the fact that her father could only express his feelings through money. She decided she could not accept the money, leaped into her car and drove straight to his house, where she had never been before. A huge row broke out in which she accused him of being responsible for all her unhappiness and lack of self-confidence. Raymond was barely able to respond, but, with the mediation of his boyfriend, father and daughter began to talk to each other for almost the first time. He discovered to his amazement that she had no bad feelings about his homosexuality, and she was equally surprised to learn that he had always loved her dearly, and it was really this love that had kept him in the unhappy marriage for so long. In the end she did get her flat, and began to see her father for enjoyable lunches together from time to time.

In expressing resentment focus on your own feelings, rather than what they are doing to you. Rehearse in your mind what you would most like to say to the person towards whom you feel resentment. Stay with your side of things: 'I feel that…', rather than 'You never…'. No one can deny you your thoughts and feelings – they are yours alone. Prepare yourself to speak your feelings. After a lifetime of suppression it may seem terrifying. The right moment never seems to come. There is always someone around, or your partner or parent is tired and in a mood. You have to make the right time happen. Prepare yourself; come back to your breathing; remain calm.

Avoid saying things in the heat of the moment which may be destructive and damaging, but do not shelve conflict for too long or the feel-

> *To overcome resentment you have to be calm but firm, respectful but determined*

ings will fester. Register your resentment and book a time when you can discuss it. Own your feelings – they originate in you, however much they are provoked by outside events – rather than projecting or blaming them on others. Accusations usually make the other person feel bad or guilty and lead to escalating conflict when he or she counter-attacks in self-defence. To overcome resentment you have to be calm but firm, respectful but determined.

Transformation

'From resentment to assertion, from accusation to disclosure of feelings.'

The spectrum of anger

Where do you fit in on this continuum ?

When I am angry I :

1. a) Take it out on everyone around me.
   b) Work out my aims before speaking to the relevant person.
2. a) Explode with rage in a way that makes things worse.
   b) Wait until I feel calm, and then make sure I express my feelings to the person who has upset me.
3. a) Bottle up my feelings of rage.
   b) Use the energy to do something constructive – chop logs, join a social action group, etc.
4. a) Secretly plan my revenge – 'I'll pay him back'.
   b) Make sure that I assert my rights.
5. a) Pretend that everything is all right.
   b) Stand my ground, remain calm, express my feelings.

CHAPTER 9
THE GREEN MOODS

ENVY

'Some folks rail against other folks, because other folks have got what some folks would be glad of.' (Fielding)

We all experience moments of envy from time to time. 'What's he (or she) got that I haven't got ?'… 'It's all right for some'… 'Some people are just born lucky'. Many people can remember the arrival of a new baby in the family when they were children. Arrival? A rival. Suddenly everyone is fussing over this noisy bundle that can't even talk, let alone play football. 'What's so special about them? What have they got…? I wish I could just lie and gurgle and cry and send everyone into such stupid ecstasy.' Of course in such moments you forget that you were a baby yourself once and, no doubt, received just as much fuss and admiration.

Envy, like its close relation, jealousy, thrives on the differences between human beings. These differences are of many kinds :

Arbitrary minor biological differences.
- Some are in themselves of no particular significance: the colour of your hair or eyes, or whether or not you like the taste of avocado.

The variability of biological endowment.
- We vary in height, intelligence, musicality and so on, and although these talents can be fostered or held back depending on circumstances, there are limits set by genetic inheritance.

Arbitrary social differences.

- A third group of differences are equally arbitrary: whether we are born into a rich country or a poor one and, within that country, which social class we belong to is a matter of pure chance. Social attitudes also affect, though they should not, the way in which we feel about biological differences; the colour of our skin is the most obvious example, gender is another.

Differences due to accident, or 'fate'.

- Some of us are plagued by misfortune, while others seem to go through life untouched by major suffering.

Changes which occur in the course of our lifetime.

- We start off small, helpless and powerless – but loveable and easily picked up and cuddled or carried. We end up comparatively big and mature and powerful – but not usually quite so adorable!

Envy latches onto one or other of these differences. As the object of your envy goes up, so you go down: 'She's got everything, good looks, a good job, money, a loving husband – and I've got nothing, nothing at all'. As you fall into a state of envy you forget everything good about yourself and become obsessed with what you are not, or have not got. The envious imagination is powerfully vivid. You picture the wonderful time they are having – glamorous holidays, a perfect sex life, lots of money – while you are stuck at home in your dreary existence. Outshone by their brilliance, any good things about you or your life pale into insignificance. You lose touch with yourself and can think only about the object of your envy. You want to be like them,

envy is almost like being in love

and the next best thing is to follow them around in your mind.

At times envy is almost like being in love: you are obsessed by the person you envy. This 'positive envy' can be an extreme form of admiration, a stimulus which can bring out the best in you. More often envy is destructive: you hate the object of your envy, and delight in their misfortunes. The person you envy is, in your mind, always bigger and better than you. You long for them to fall off their smug perch, you are always on the look out for any scraps of information that may suggest they are not so perfect as they appear, and if things do go wrong for them you are overjoyed. There is nothing you would like better than to see them cut down to size. Like the dog in the manger, even though what they have got is no use to you, you will do your utmost to prevent them enjoying it.

Envy and jealousy are not synonymous, although there is a great overlap in the way the words are commonly used – including the way we use them in this chapter. Envy usually involves two people, while jealousy, which often refers to sexual possessiveness, involves three people – you, your partner (real or imagined), and someone you imagine would like to deprive you of them. If your partner is chatting to an attractive member of the opposite sex at a party you may be envious of the other person's looks, vivacity or intelligence, but jealous of the attention and interest your partner is bestowing on them.

Envy springs from insecurity and fragile self-esteem. In a state of envy you cease to believe in yourself, and endow the object of your envy with all the ideal attributes that you would like to possess yourself. At the root of this is the feeling that you are not lovable. You then start to think 'If… I was more like her (or him), then they would really notice me, love me, want to be with me…'. The more low in self-worth you are, the more vulnerable to envious feelings.

Envy can be traced back to childhood, and especially to feelings towards brothers and sisters, who, if they weren't younger and getting all the attention, were older and getting all the perks. And if you were an only child you envied those lucky people who belonged to huge happy families. Sibling envy, based on minute differences often unnoticeable to other people, can go on for a lifetime, simmering in the background, but quickly brought to a full rolling boil over issues such as inheritance.

EXAMPLE: THE INHERITORS

Sukie was a mature, confident, successful TV producer in her fifties, happily married with self-motivated and interesting children. As a child she and her sister had each been close to one parent – she to her father, her sister to her mother. Her father, an artist, had died of a heart attack when she was only 16. Soon after this she had left home, much against her mother's wishes, and it was only in later years that she and her mother became reconciled. When her mother died, Sukie and her sister met to divide up her estate, which included hundreds of her father's pictures. Sukie found a wave of furious rage come over her when her sister claimed one particularly fine painting which she insisted had been promised her by their mother. Before she knew what was happening, Sukie was howling and shouting at her sister, just as she had as a child. It took several months before the absurdity of wanting just one out of the huge number of pictures came home to her, and her resentment and feeling of unfairness wore off.

Despite the universality of envy most people manage to cope with the basic unfairness of life – although this does not mean that they would not like to see, or take active steps to promote, a more equitable society. This may be because they had the good fortune to grow up in a family in which children had no cause to envy the power and privileges of their parents, and siblings were helped to feel that, despite temporary advantage or disadvantage, each one got what he or she needed as an individual.

Suggestions

Start by trying to recognize the part envy plays in your life: 'Hello envy'. Don't be afraid of it. It is a normal and natural feeling. It is also much more widespread than many people admit. Try to monitor fleeting feelings of envy as they happen to you through the day. When you are bitching about someone in the office, or reading avidly in the papers about the discomfiture of royalty or the downfall of politicians, are you motivated by envy ?

Once you have identified your envy, try to 'sit' on it, touch it, look deeply into it. What feelings of hurt, exclusion and neglect lie beneath it? Did you perhaps feel that your mother always favoured boys rather than girls, and does this affect your relationship with your partner? Did you as a child feel that you could never live up to your parents' expectations of you as the ideal offspring? Does your envy spring from a wish to be perfect, as you imagine the object of your envy to be, in the hope that this will finally bring you the unconditional love you are seeking? Perhaps your parents had feelings of inadequacy which made it so important to them that you should be perfect? Did your mother, for instance, deal with her own oppression as a woman by idealizing boys, thus always making you, as a girl, feel second-best and envious of males, with potentially damaging effects on your relationships with men ?

Turn your envy into admiration – 'positive envy'. The person you envy is someone you could learn from. Let them have their qualities, be generous in your feelings towards them, feel enriched by them. Rather than feeling empty and useless and 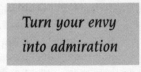 inadequate, begin to value your own qualities for what they are. You are good enough. Accept yourself: you are all you can or ever will be. You are a complete and perfect being, different from others but neither inferior nor superior. A primrose is not

Turn your envy into admiration

inferior to a bluebell – just different. Envy is destructive. By cutting the object of your envy down to size you may feel better temporarily, but then you will begin to feel guilty about what you have done, and this will start up the vicious circle of envy again as you compare your guilty 'bad' self with the imagined goodness of others.

You inflate the object of your envy with all sorts of imagined advantages. If their position changes – they become seriously ill, or lose a child – you may suddenly perceive them as a sister or brother human, struggling, vulnerable and in need of the caring support you have to offer.

EXAMPLE: SCHOOL FRIENDS

Camilla and Jane were best friends at school. They did everything together, and spent most of the holidays in each other's houses. Camilla's parents – who were divorced – were much better off than Jane's, but that did not seem to matter. The girls seemed to complement one another. Camilla was full of excitement and fun, while Jane provided a nurturing quality that Camilla seemed to lack. When Jane married soon after leaving school, Camilla came to live with her friend and husband and new baby as a lodger. After a few years Camilla met and married a promising businessman. They moved into a beautiful house, Camilla started to have babies and to live an apparently ideal and happy family life with her ever more successful husband and delightful children. Jane continued seeing her, but as her marriage started to founder she began to feel increasingly inadequate when she visited Camilla, who paraded her husband's and children's latest successes before her. Soon Camilla herself began to achieve her own success running a successful fashion business. Jane began to feel more and more dowdy and a failure. At first she was angry with herself for feeling envious, but after a while she realized that Camilla's behaviour was perhaps deliberately (if unconsciously) provoking envy as well. Camilla seemed to need to be envied if she was to feel good herself. Things came to a head when Camilla reported to Jane that her stepmother had said that she 'didn't quite see the point of Jane!' After this Jane resolved to have less to do with Camilla and they drifted apart. Some years later Camilla's husband became seriously ill, his business collapsed, and Jane heard that Camilla was very depressed. She contacted her and they arranged to meet. Camilla was able to talk about some of her miseries and insecurities. Jane's envy, and Camilla's envy-provocation, had vanished.

It is important to identify the the sources of your envy. Like Camilla, some people can be envy-provoking as they parade their perfect marriages, successful children, smoothly running careers and glamorous holidays before you. Perhaps, in spite of all these advantages, they still feel inadequate and dissatisfied and need to feed their fragile self-esteem with your envy. Similarly, envy-producing advertisements on TV depict the idyllic lifestyles of perfectly happy families in tasteful, orderly houses where plentiful food is greeted by happy and appreciative children who all have slim figures yet are apparently able to gorge on endless sweets. See these for the dreams they are. If it helps, think about the tired actress doing her umpteenth 'take' and pretending to look happy when in reality she is bored, longing for a cup of tea, surrounded by frenetic cameramen, in a boiling hot and overlit studio, skin taut with makeup concealing every human blemish. Try to see that your own envy is far from unique – even the person you envy may suffer from it.

EXAMPLE: THE ENVY OF THE ENVIED

Richard was thrown into a state of confusion when a senior colleague, whom he greatly envied for his reputation, salary and ability, came to stay for the night. To his amazement, this colleague then spent much of his time complaining to Richard about the unjustified reputation of a colleague senior to him and speculating about how he came so effortlessly by his acclaim! This did much to cure Richard of his envy and helped him to laugh at his own ambition and vain sense of rivalry, because he saw that he and his colleagues were like a flock of hens with their pecking order.

Finally, we can learn much from our envy. In it are the seeds of an ideal to which we aspire and which can help us to value the good qualities which we have and try harder to achieve those we seek. At the same time, if we can penetrate our envy we will realize that reality is never ideal, that it is our very imperfection that makes us whole, that struggle and loss and change are what makes life meaningful and interesting. A plastic rose will never be an adequate substitute for a real one, even though the real one will fade and its petals will fall. The Persian carpet makers always included a deliberate imperfection in their work, partly to remind people that only God is perfect, but also perhaps because they intuitively knew that there is ultimately something unsatisfying about too much perfection.

Transformation
'My envy leads me to appreciate and value my true self, to accept my imperfections.'

CONTEMPT

'Whenever we pretend… a mighty contempt for anything, it is a clear sign that we feel ourselves very nearly on a level with it.' (Hazlitt)

Contempt looks down from a great height. 'There were many subjects in the world – perhaps the majority – in which she felt no interest, because they were stupid'. Gwendolen, the 20-year- old heroine of George Eliot's *Daniel Deronda*, exemplifies the sweeping dismissal of the unknown and unfamiliar, characteristic of some adolescents. As children we may have felt looked down upon or dismissed. Now, as adults, the tables are turned and we despise the world that was so contemptuous of us.

Underneath our contempt lurks fear. There is so much we know nothing about. We are threatened by our ignorance. We cling to what we know,

> *Underneath our contempt lurks fear*

reject with contempt whatever seems alien and strange. We enjoy mocking and despising the way other people dress, spend their money, pronounce words, celebrate their religion. Often this is harmless and amusing – human behaviour is enormously variable – and in our laughter there is also a recognition and a basic acceptance of these endless differences which exist between groups of people. But our mocking laughter is not far from contempt, beyond which lie the malignant blind forces of prejudice, intolerance and hatred.

Contempt is in the eye of the beholder. A chrysalis looks uninteresting and 'boring' – but once we think of the splendour of the emerging moth or butterfly it becomes precious and full of potential. A pregnant woman may look fat and cumbersome to some, but she is magnificent and touchingly beautiful to those who are aware of the full cycle of life and birth and death. Would Gwendolen be delighted by the first faltering steps of her one-year-old child, or would she find him 'stupid' also? Just as adolescents despise the dreary opinions and unfashionable clothes of their parents' generation, so old people dismiss the gaudy regalia of the young.

Underlying contempt there is often envy. By belittling, or even wishing to destroy, the object of our contempt we are no longer at the mercy of our desire for it, and also deprive others of its pleasures. We feel superior, 'above such things', artificially bolstering our fragile self-esteem at the expense of another's.

Suggestions

Observe yourself as you judge others, think critical thoughts, make censorious or 'bitchy' comments. It is surprising how many of our interactions with people are infected with minor forms of contempt. Focus on your need to build yourself up as 'better' than others, while avoiding the trap of despising yourself for being so contemptuous! You are only human – as frail and fearful and vulnerable as the next person. Ask yourself if what you despise in the other does not contain some germ of what you would really like for yourself. If you are young, you may wish you had some of the stability and experience and settledness of age; if you are older, perhaps you envy the freedom and optimism of the young.

Brood on the object of your contempt. Are you attacking some part of yourself that you dislike and have conveniently located in someone else? If you bemoan the conformity of the young – why do they all have to wear their hair the same way, use the same dreadful lingo, listen to the same cacophonous music? – perhaps you are fretting inside the straightjacket of your safe job, mortgage, marriage. Think positively about the differences between people, the variety that contributes so richly to our success as a species and to the beauty and excitement of life. No two people are are exactly the same – however much they try to be. Long live differences!

Transformation
'In what I despise I find a lost part of myself .'

GREED

'Big mouthfuls often choke.' (Italian proverb)

Greed is based on wanting too much of a good thing. Like most 'bad' moods the basis of greed is imbalance. We all need good food to eat, money to buy

> *wanting too much of a good thing*

things, recognition of our own value. In a state of greed the equilibrium within ourselves, between us and those near us, and with our environment is disturbed. We fill ourselves with food until our bellies hurt and we can't move comfortably. We want more and more money even though we have quite enough. We crave power and success. Greed is a one-way traffic. We take and take, but cannot give back. We feel deprived, so we deprive others. We cannot balance our need with gratitude or generosity. We eat inessential food as we watch people dying of starvation in Africa. We despoil the environment so as to meet our insatiable greed for minerals. The rain forest is destroyed in the scramble to become hamburger millionaires.

EXAMPLE: THE FISHERMAN'S WIFE

We are like the fisherman's wife in the fairy tale whose husband saves the life of a magic fish which in return offers to grant him any wish. First his wife wants a bigger house, then she insists on a mansion. Still dissatisfied, she demands a palace. Even this is not enough; she finally wishes to have power over the winds and tides. Now her greed has gone too far; disgusted, the fish returns her to her humble hut by the seashore.

Greed prevents us from enjoying what we have – like the fisherman's wife, the more we have the more we want. As sufferers from alcoholism or bulimia know, it is the first step that counts. One little drink, just one biscuit – and you are roaring drunk or have consumed a fridgeful of food.

If feeding is the model on which all greed is based, then our first lessons come from our parents. Some will be ever-giving, stuffing the baby with breast or bottle at every opportunity and interpreting every whimper as a sign of hunger. This child is being taught that whenever she feels bad there is always comfort in food or drink – sowing the seed of greed in which bad feelings are met with food, leading to more bad feelings, further guzzling and so on. At the other end of the spectrum are parents who strictly regulate their baby's feeds both in time and quantity. This child may grow up never feeling quite satisfied. There has never been quite enough to give her a warm full feeling. This may lead to a self split into two parts, in which one eats in a polite restrained way, while the other is ravenously given to guilty moments of secret indulgence.

Suggestions

Distinguish between need and greed. You have a right to have your needs met and are far more likely to be giving and generous to others if you feel valued and satisfied. Greed is often a by-product of lack of satisfaction, and the way to over-

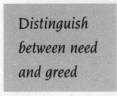

Distinguish between need and greed

come it is not by denial but by being loving and generous to yourself. Find the real hunger within your greed and try to feed that. Perhaps your greed is an expression not of craving for food but of loneliness or insecurity.

Find an image for your greed. Is it a gaping maw? A sucking leech? Shearing shark's teeth? A huge hungry baby? A millionaire who can have every bodily need satisfied at the flick of his fingers? 'Hullo greed'. Try making the image grow bigger and smaller in size until it is just the right distance from you so that you don't feel overwhelmed by it. Tell your greedy self that it can have an occasional blow-out – feast days are important, if only to get the measure of our greed for the rest of the year.

Find the real need that lies behind the greed. Your wish for money may be based on a need for independence and freedom. Wanting a bigger house may reflect feelings of insecurity. Your craving for success may be to do with a lack of belief in yourself and your inherent lovability. Each of these wishes needs to be taken seriously. If your greed has led to you to tackle them then it is to be welcomed.

EXAMPLE: NEVER SATISFIED

Anthony was a successful barrister who ascended his career ladder with remarkable speed – first class honours, distinction in his law exams, top legal firm, QC. Yet with each achievement he felt little satisfaction – just a hollow feeling of anti-climax as he started to think about the next hurdle. He always wanted more, and could not understand or overcome his continuing sense of emptiness and inadequacy. He was haunted by the feeling that he would be 'found out' to be an ordinary and pedestrian person rather than the success the world took him for. Brooding on the theme of 'achievement' he remembered the deathbed rebuke of his grandfather (himself a highly intelligent man who had left school at 14 and had made a great success in business): 'Anthony, I am disappointed in you – I always thought to see you a judge before I died'. He then pictured his mother, an emotionally distant woman who had suffered from anorexia nervosa – her father had never quite recovered from his disappointment that she was not a boy – and who had had huge ambitions for him, having suppressed her own intellectual abilities for the sake of her children and married a man very different from her father, sensitive but unambitious. He then saw how the family pattern of 'greed' was working itself out through him, and that his constant need for ever more success was a diversion from an unsatisfied longing for intimacy and love that he – and his mother before him – lacked as a child.

Exercise: A mindful meal

Whether or not your greed centres around food, make a time for a 'mindful meal'. (This is not as easy as it seems.) Choose the most wholesome delicious ingredients that will nourish your body. Even if you are going to eat the meal alone, prepare it as you would for the most honoured guest. Arrange the table or tray beautifully. Put a beautiful bouquet of flowers on it. You deserve this degree of respect. When you eat, keep your mind on the food and chew it slowly, savouring and thinking about each mouthful. Turn off the radio or TV and, if you are with your family, eat this special meal in silence. Where was the food grown? How has it reached your plate from all the different parts of the world? Think with gratitude of the many hands and arms and backs that have gone into growing and transporting it. Think of the sun and the rain and the soil and how we too are interdependent with our environment. Visualize the food feeding you, filling you, satisfying your vital needs, and how the purity and freshness of the food is benefiting your body. Think too of the one third of the earth's population who lack adequate food and clean water. In these ways you will have transformed your greed into healthy hunger and, once satisfied, will be better able to contribute to the meeting of other people's needs.

Transformation
'From greed to need; from anxious craving to healthy hunger.'

JEALOUSY

'The dragon that slays love under the pretence of keeping it alive.' (Havelock Ellis)

A jealous person is a zealot – from which the word jealous derives – vigilant in guarding what he has got, ever fearful that it will be snatched from him. Unlike envy, which desires what others have and would dearly love to have for itself, jealousy is about what you feel is yours by right but has been, or is about to be, snatched from you. Often the two overlap – as children we are both envious and jealous of our siblings who not only steal the parental attention which we desire, but also, in our envious eyes, have the characteristics – being cleverer or stronger, male rather than female – which enable them to claim parental preference.

Living with jealousy is uncomfortable. You can never fully relax for fear that everything good will be taken from you while your guard is down. You are constantly struggling with the wish to possess, and the fear that in doing so you may lose or destroy what you have. The more locks and burglar alarms you put on your house, the more tempting a target it may appear to burglars. If you suffer from sexual jealousy any conversation with your partner is full of danger. He has only to mention the name of an attractive girl in the office, or she a former boyfriend whom she is still 'friends' with, for you to feel a cold chill run through you. You feel rebuffed and inadequate. Going to a party can be a misery as you watch your partner laughing, gently resting his or her hand on someone else. You feel betrayed and forgotten. They laugh enthusiastically – fool that you were, you thought that it was only you that could amuse and entertain your lover.

If jealousy takes hold, you punish your partner with your sulks and accusations. You demand to know every detail of their day. If they are reluctant to talk, that feeds your suspicions. You protest if they have to go anywhere alone. You punish them for their imagined faithlessness by starting up a flirtation yourself. They in turn feel rejected, or start to tire of your possessiveness and really begin to look elsewhere for love and understanding. Your worst suspicions are confirmed. You have succeeded in creating with your jealousy the very outcome you feared.

The roots of your jealousy often lie in childhood insecurities. Perhaps your mother favoured boys – when they did something naughty she would be amused, but when you did much the same you met with her disapproval and righteous anger. In your eyes your mother seemed so fickle – you could never rest secure in her love, if you were out of her sight she would forget you. Perhaps your parents were divorced and your father had a series of girlfriends who always seemed to interest him more than you, his mere daughter, did. What power do you have against such rivals? These same anxieties then affect your adult relationships.

EXAMPLE: OTHELLO AND DESDEMONA

Othello is the epitome of jealousy. Iago played on his insecurity and through this persuaded him that his devoted and loving wife Desdemona was being unfaithful to him. The origins of his insecurity lay in the traumatic separation from his family, in which he was a prince, when he was snatched away to become a slave at the age of seven. Despite his great success and acclaim as a military commander in Venice, he felt vulnerable and insecure about his position as a prominent black man in a white and racist Venetian society. He was easy prey for Iago.

Suggestions

In jealousy all your thoughts are concentrated away from your-self on the real or feared loss. You are acutely aware of the ways in which your rival is favoured, of how other men or women find your partner attractive. Rather than making you feel pleased for their sake, or flattered for your own, this touches a raw nerve in your precarious self-esteem, though this is the last thing you are aware of. To transform feelings of jealousy you need, with the help of breathing, to return to yourself and to the anxiety and low self-esteem which underlie it.

There may well be a valid basis to your feelings. Maybe your partner cannot commit him- or herself fully to your relation-ship, which fuels your feelings of worthlessness and insecurity. But total possession is in any case an impossibility, and possessiveness will feel to your partner like a trap, not a safe haven. When you start to focus on the impact your jealousy is having on your own well-being, you may decide that you cannot continue while your relationship is so uncertain.

Action of some sort will in itself make you feel a little better. You have had the courage to risk loss for the sake of a better relation-ship. Mood-brood your jealousy. Picture to yourself in your inner dialogue the hurt

> **Think of the many good things about your life – of what you have got, rather than what you lack**

and rejection you feel, the sense of being cast aside and inad-equate. In your state of jealousy you feel 'If only he were faith-ful, then I would be all right'. Concentrate instead on giving yourself the love and attention you really need. Say to yourself 'I am an important and creative person. I have a right to fulfil my potential'. Think of the many good things about your life – of what you have got, rather than what you lack: good health, supportive friends, some money in the bank at least. With the help of your breathing, bring yourself into the fullness of the present moment, and away from the imaginary, empty future with which your jealousy so cunningly deludes you.

Transformation
'Not empty and lacking, but full of hidden gifts waiting to be realized.'

MISTRUST

'I have seen flowers come in stony places
And kind things done by men with ugly faces,
And the gold cup won by the worst horse at the races.'
(John Masefield)

When we mistrust we lose faith in our fellow human beings. How can we be sure that smile was well meant, that kiss genuine? People flatter to deceive, to deprive us of what is rightfully ours. They are not really interested in us, just in what they can get out of us.

EXAMPLE: TO SMILE AND BE A VILLAIN

In the contemporary classic Chinese film, *Raise the Red Lantern*, set in the 1920s in China, a young student reluctantly enters a patriarch's household as 'fourth mistress'. 'Third mistress' is openly hostile and rivalrous and uses all her ruses to keep the master to herself. 'Second mistress' is all smiles to the newcomer and showers her with presents. But it is she who has secretly made a wax effigy of 'fourth mistress' and is sticking pins into it. 'Fear the Greeks even when they bring presents' is the watchword for the mistrustful.

In a state of mistrust we sense a wall of hostility when we enter a room full of people. Either we feel invisible as they turn away and appear not to notice our presence or, worse still, they laugh at us, whispering spiteful remarks to their friends behind their hands. Mistrustful, we approach others with extreme caution, matching their imagined hostility with defensiveness or dissembling. In the grip of paranoia we decide that it is better to assume in advance that we will be let down, rather than to risk rejection or exploitation. How can we ever be sure that our neighbour isn't out to humiliate or take advantage of us?

Mistrust has two main origins. The first is the actual experience of rejection, neglect or ill-treatment. For the cruelly beaten dog, his master is a potential source of further pain. Mistrust often has its roots in childhood events which may be long forgotten (locked away with other painful memories) in which parents, although not necessarily wilfully cruel, may through preoccupation with their own problems have neglected or even abused their children. Such children when they grow up may find it hard to believe that they will not be ridiculed or abandoned if they reveal their feelings. Another related source of mistrust depends on 'projection'. Here you attribute to others all the negative feelings which you feel yourself. For example, if you feel threatened by meeting new people, you will assume that they dislike you and so behave in a defensive way; this in turn may actually cause the rejection which you expected to receive in the first place. Mistrust breeds more mistrust and so becomes self-perpetuating.

Suggestions

Trust requires an act of faith and the capacity to contain our natural anxieties and to see them for what they are. When we swim in the sea we trust that there will be no sharks, that our body knows how to float and to protect us from the cold. Extreme pain in childhood – such as that set up by childhood

> **Think to yourself 'I *am* valuable, not vulnerable'**

abuse – destroys the mental capacity for self-protection and therefore any situation of intimacy is approached with great caution in case it leads to more exploitation. Once you have met a shark it takes enormous courage to go swimming again. So an important part of overcoming mistrust is to feel that we can defend ourselves or remove ourselves from danger should the need arise. Think to yourself 'I am valuable, not vulnerable – no longer a helpless child but a strong adult who has a right not to be hurt, who can leave situations if they are damaging, and who has a lot of strength to withstand pain'. You may need to enhance your physical self-confidence in a practical way: by going to keep fit classes or learning self-defence or a martial art. This can make you more courageous and lessen your need to mistrust.

Focus on your negative feelings towards other people: your hostility, envy, wish to humiliate. How much do you attribute these feelings to those whom you mistrust? Is your mistrust based on misperception? Is it possible that your own attitude is bringing out the very rejection which you fear? If you treat someone as a potential enemy he may well become one, whereas if you treat him as a friend he may respond to that – and even if he does not, you are strong enough to withstand his betrayal. When you are let down by people – as inevitably happens from time to time – find a way to express appropriate anger towards them. Let them know how hurt you feel. Try to understand, without necessarily condoning, their behaviour. 'Sit' on someone who you feel has hurt you. Think about them from a broad perspective. Perhaps they themselves were the victims of rejection or abuse, or have been hurt by you.

Exercise: Trust in the canteen

Try an 'automatic thoughts' experiment. Make a list of the situations and people you mistrust. Arrange them in order from greatest to least threat. Take one of the least worrying situations and imagine yourself in it. Write down the automatic thoughts that come up in you in such a situation. Perhaps it is the canteen at lunchtime. You feel people don't really want to sit next to you. Automatic thoughts come into your mind: 'I am a boring person', 'They all know each other, they've no time for a newcomer like me', 'It's completely hopeless – I'll never be able to make friends'. Ask yourself how strongly you believe that to be true. Challenge your automatic thoughts. Perhaps they just don't know you, or are shy themselves, or are in awe of you. How much is others' behaviour a function of the way you treat them? As an experiment be friendly to someone you mistrust. Have the courage to be the one who makes the first move.

Transformation

'Mistrust shows up how my misperception of the world colours experience, and leads me to perceive myself and things for what they are.'

The spectrum of envy and jealousy

Where do you place yourself ?

When I am envious/jealous I :

1   a) Secretly wish harm to the other person.
    b) Turn the object of my envy into a model I
    aspire to.

2   a) Feel diminished, belittled and rejected.
    b) Think how my envy may be coloured by
    childhood memories.

3   a) Seek out others who share my dislike of the
    envied person – 'Let's all hate...'
    b) If I feel that my situation is truly unfair, claim
    what I believe to be my rights rather than
    harbouring grudges.

4   a) Conceal my feelings of inadequacy with pretence
    and deceit.
    b) Recognize and accept envy and the part it plays
    in my life.

5   a) Do my utmost to provoke envy in others.
    b) Acknowledge that everyone is differently
    endowed with a variety of talents and capacities.

CHAPTER 10
MOODS AND MAJOR TRAUMA

'The butterfly counts not months but moments and

has time enough.' (Tagore)

One of the main themes of this book is that it is not so much what happens to us that determines our moods as our attitude towards events – 'men are troubled not so much by things as by their appreciation of things'. If we can face the losses and setbacks and disappointments of life without either denying our feelings or being overwhelmed by them, we can deepen and strengthen our relationship to the world.

This is all very well perhaps for the 'ordinary' misfortunes that fate brings most of us, but what about the really devastating blows that befall some people? Surely these cannot be coped with by a mere change of attitude ?

It is certainly true that people who have escaped major trauma are, on the whole, less likely to be troubled by anxiety and depression than those who have not escaped such unhappiness. But that is by no means the whole story. Someone who has had his share of love and openness, and has had to overcome some major difficulty, such as blindness or a degenerative disease may be 'steeled' by the experience and so be more resilient than those whose lives have been entirely sheltered. Helen Keller and Stephen Hawking are two famous examples of this phenomenon. Security comes not so much from the avoidance of suffering but from the ability to express the grief and anger which go with pain and to look at one's life-story without fear.

In this chapter we look at two of the most devastating events a person can have to endure: sexual abuse and untimely bereavement. We hope to show that even in these extreme cases the approach we have been putting forward can be of benefit. We have repeatedly stressed the importance of breathing, imagination, and naming.

Breathing is your great protector. As you breathe you calm your anxiety, you replenish your strength, you focus on your whole self, you are linked with the air which nourishes and supports you and without which you could not live for more than a few minutes. However damaged your body, your breathing remains intact.

EXAMPLE: BREATHING THE SAME AIR

Ruth had been sexually and physically abused as a child and felt that all the portals of her body were contaminated. She could not enjoy kissing or making love: her mouth and genitals were sullied. Even eating was hard. She imagined herself taking the security and goodness of her therapist in through her breath, and this thought calmed her. When, despite this, she still felt abandoned and un-nurtured she was helped by her therapist's reminder that they were both breathing the same air: what she breathed out he took in, and vice versa.

Your imagination can put you in touch with the power and control you can have over your inner world, however lost and helpless you may feel in relation to the outer world. Whatever cruelty fate deals you, you are still free to imagine, to dream, to fantasize. But imagination is a two-edged sword. You can hide away from the horrors of reality in a world of make-believe, but using your creative powers can also be vital in your recovery from trauma.

Putting your feelings into words can also be central to recovery from both sexual abuse and loss. The disclosure of sexual abuse is the first step towards facing what has happened. Talking about loss – in your own words, at your own pace and in your own time – is the beginning of the long road towards relinquishing the pain of grief.

Time plays an important part both in the impact of trauma and recovery from it. When we have a major shock time comes to a standstill. We are petrified at the moment the blow fell. We return constantly in our mind to the image of the abuse. We are imprisoned in the past, cannot be in the present or look towards the future. But, as healing takes place, we are gradually released from the trap of the past. Seeing how our lives are part of a changing cycle of growth, maturity and decay, little by little, our pain can begin to fall into some kind of pattern and to become more bearable. As we feel more integrated, our inner rhythms re-assert themselves. The scars remain, but hope and truth become once more a possibility.

Suggestions for relieving some of the pain of abuse

'The sun, though it passes through dirty places, yet remains as pure as before.' (Francis Bacon)

When we hear of someone who is suffering or has suffered from exploitation or abuse, our hearts are touched. We want to hold, cradle and protect this person whose innocence and trust have been so cruelly violated. We long to heal the wounds that have been inflicted, to contact the seeds of trust and purity within that person, to nurture and nourish them.

Yet for a victim it is usually impossible at first, and always hard, to accept such help. The abused child within is likely to be withdrawn, mistrustful, angry and defensive. How can anyone be trusted when those who were supposed to care for you, protect you and love you have failed to do so ?

If you have been abused there will be many contradictory feelings within you. You will feel fear: fear of looking at what really happened, fear that to do so will remind you of the terror you felt then. You will feel hatred and disgust, which properly belong to the person who abused you, but which you may feel towards yourself as though you were in some way to blame for what happened. You will, somewhere, also feel an enormous need for the love and care and protection which, had it been present then, would have saved you from what happened. This need may be deeply buried so that you are unable to get close to people, or all too near the surface making you desperately seek out any reassurance you can. The first leaves you feeling lost and hollow inside. The second exposes you to the possibility of further exploitation and abuse.

Examine closely your feelings of outrage and repulsion. It can be helpful to write an account of what happened – this helps to objectify your feelings. Draw a picture illustrating your abused self and your feelings about whoever it was that abused you. This may be particularly confusing if it was a parent whom at one level you loved and trusted. Perhaps you see yourself as a little grey mouse, timid and tiny, with a huge cat torturing you, playing with you, tossing you around for sport and amusement. Visualize or draw this cruel beast as it felt and feels to you. Then put a barrier between the victim and the aggressor: a wall or a trap or a cage. You are free and safe – but your aggressor needs to remain locked up or he may turn to other prey if you put yourself beyond his reach. Get in touch with the part of you that may have felt that it was your duty to sacrifice yourself, either for your aggressor's sake (you may be only too aware of the weakness and vulnerability which lies behind his cruelty), or to protect others who would otherwise have been attacked.

Exercise: The circle of safety

You may need to imagine layer upon layer of confinement until you begin to feel at all secure. The aggressor must be bound and gagged, locked in a dungeon, in a castle, surrounded by a deep moat. Or, like the leaking reactor at Chernobyl, encased in thick concrete and put out of bounds. Allow yourself to be safe. You will need the help of others. Picture yourself as part of a circle, holding hands with all those whom you trust and who trust you. Sense the strength of shared good feelings and mutual concern and love. Release the concern and love you feel for them, it will help your own healing process. Those in your circle accept and love you as you are, whatever has happened to you, however you feel about yourself. Your experiences may have cut you off from other people, so it may be hard to find the friends with whom to share your pain, even in your imagination. Draw on past memories of kind, caring people, even if they have died or are no longer part of your life: teachers, neighbours, grannies, aunts, a friendly postman or a pet which was special to you. Lose your sense of yourself as a separate person. In your circle you all make one safe whole – a ring of strength, acceptance and love. You are an essential part of this ring; together you form a whole united group. If you feel empty, damaged, incomplete, let the generosity of the circle refill you. Draw on the stream of concern to nourish the parched desert of your feelings.

Focus on your breath during the visualization. Breathe in purity; breathe out shame and disgust. With your in-breath feel a clear stream of pure air enter you; release your violated feelings with your out-breath.

In abuse bad feelings are rooted deep in the body as well as the mind. Your body will contain feelings of bruising and defilement long after the abuse has ceased. After making yourself relaxed and breathing steadily in a warm place (perhaps in the bath) imagine a cleansing current gently caressing you and washing away the stain and the stench and the hurt. Your whole body and especially the parts that have been violated feel renewed and made whole by this process. Repeat this visualization until you regain some sense of integrity and self-respect.

Eventually you may come to a point where you want to confront your aggressor. Imagine yourself with the tables turned, making them suffer the hurt and self-hatred you have gone through. If you feel murderous – allow these feelings to come freely into your mind. Notice the subtle ways in which you attack your partner or those to whom you are close, communicating your suffering by inflicting pain upon them. It is natural that you should behave so, and it may give you an insight into your own aggressor. Perhaps he was abused, abandoned, bullied, deprived in the past. Think of him as the small helpless child he once was, going through something similar to what he has perpetrated on you. See the way in which cycles of abuse transmit themselves down the generations. Resolve to break the pattern – and be lenient towards yourself for your inevitable mistakes and setbacks.

Suggestions for living with loss

'Give sorrow words: the grief that does not speak
Whispers the o'er-fraught heart, and bids it break.' (Macbeth)

Grief is the inevitable result of loss, however and whenever it comes. Sadness, mental pain, searching, anger, feelings of emptiness and confusion, tears, sleeplessness, self-questioning – these are all normal parts of the grief response. They may take us unawares, even if the loss is timely and we are well prepared for it. Just as our bodies have evolved a series of responses to physical injury which ensures that a breach in our skin is repaired – bleeding, clotting, swelling, redness, knitting together, regrowth, scarring – so too with the psychological hole that opens up when someone we are close to dies or leaves us.

Unheralded loss, as when your partner leaves you suddenly and without warning, is a body blow to your self-esteem, especially if they have left you for someone else. All the expectations and habits around which you have built your life are threatened to the core. Perhaps you feel it would have been easier if your partner had died; at least then the painful and confusing feelings of grief would not be compounded by jealousy, and uncertainty.

EXAMPLE: SUDDENLY A WIDOW

Pat and Frank had had many difficulties in their marriage and she had often thought of leaving him. One day she was preparing Sunday lunch while her husband and eldest son were out jogging together. Suddenly she had a distraught telephone call: 'Dad's in hospital – he collapsed while we were running.' By the time she arrived Frank had died. She experienced many contradictory feelings – shock and disorientation at the loss of her partner of 20 years, fear at having to help her children through their grief on her own, fury at being abandoned with three children and a large mortgage, guilt about all the imperfections in the relationship. She grieved intensely, and several years later formed a new relationship, but retained a strong sense of Frank's presence: 'He's always with me, helping me and encouraging me.'

Even for a grown-up the death of a parent is often a devastating blow. The normal patterns of your life are swept aside by a tide of grief. If both have died you are now 'nobody's child', childlike in your vulnerability, and yet never more adult as you face your own death without the buffering of your parents.

EXAMPLE: JANE'S MUM

Jane's mother, Pam, came from a poor family, and when her own mother (Jane's grandmother) died young she had to leave school to look after her five younger brothers and sisters, despite considerable academic promise, while her father continued to work as a long-distance lorry driver. Eventually Pam married and had three children of her own, who inherited her intellectual abilities. Pam delighted in her children's many achievements; tragically she died suddenly from a rare virus when Jane, her youngest daughter, was at university. When Jane had her first novel accepted her first thought was – 'I must phone Mum, she'll be over the moon.' Suddenly she remembered – there was no mum there to phone, and felt overwhelmed with sadness and disappointment.

THE DEATH OF A CHILD

Perhaps the most painful of all untimely deaths is the loss of child. Suddenly your child or baby is dead – an illness, an accident, or a cot death. You find yourself wandering in an alien world, disorientated, surrounded by strangeness and confusion, all familiar points of reference gone. You have lost the complacency of 'normality' – the state in which we are mistakenly lulled into a sense of false security. But now you are forced to feel the impermanence, fragility and mortality of every living thing.

Your instinct for self-preservation forces you to struggle to the surface, to gasp for air in order to survive, but part of you may wish to join your beloved one in death, to abandon life, to bury yourself with him or her in the ground. But you know that he (or she) is no longer there, his body just a husk that will disintegrate now that the life has left it. We invest so much in our children, we want the best for them, perhaps all the opportunities and privileges that we missed. They are young and energetic and we expect them to carry the baton forward in the relay of the generations. To lose a child feels contrary to the laws of nature. But nature is cruel – so much wastage, buds caught in a late frost, newborn lambs dying of hypothermia in the cold rain, the millions of seeds lost for the one that will become a tree. For all our sophisticated medicines and doctors and hospitals none of us are immune from this process of waste.

Searching, Grieving, Hoping

When we lose someone we love we endlessly search for them hoping against hope that there has been some mistake. We may feel very angry – angry with the driver who caused the death, with the doctor who failed to save him or her, with the loved one for exposing him- or herself to danger, with yourself for failing to protect as a parent or partner. If someone you love has taken his own life you may be plunged into appalling feelings of guilt and remorse – you were not good enough, you were rejecting, preoccupied, selfish, you berate yourself. When someone dies you are confronted by your own murderous feelings, often in a distorted and exaggerated form. You may imagine that your feelings of hate are so powerful that they can kill. Bereaved children are particularly prone to feel that it was their fault, when really their feelings were those of normal rivalry towards brothers and sisters or anger and disappointment towards parents who have frustrated their desires.

You need to unearth your lost hopes and wishes. Repossess them – they belong to you. Give to yourself the love and concern you gave or wanted to give to the person you have lost. Imagine him or her looking at you, wishing you to be joyful and loving, alive and generous, rather than burying everything good and positive in the grave.

Let your tears flow feely, but also know when to dry your tears and smile. In George Herbert's words, 'Learn weeping and thou shalt regain laughing.' Think about the happiness you shared, not just about the sadness of imagined future happiness that is not to be.

Think about time differently. Consciousness inhabits the present moment. Give yourself the time you need to attend to your grief in a focused and unhurried way. Stay with your feelings. Comfort yourself with warmth and solitude, the clothes and photographs and belongings and 'things' that remind you of your loved one.

When you are not engaged in this work of mourning, try to set your grief to one side for a while. You may be frightened to let go, for fear of reliving the shock of the loss once again. Sleep may be a problem for the same reason – you may dream of the person you have lost alive and then have to face the empty void of absence when you wake.

You will at times feel depleted and unable to give to all those who continue to need you – your work, children, partner, parents, pets and plants. Take the memory of the lost one inside yourself. Absorb all the good feelings of spontaneity, humour, liveliness, creativity – make these your own, they are the legacy left you by the one who has died.

When we are bereaved we are prisoners of time. The dying Richard the Second says, too late, 'I wasted time and now doth time waste me.' If only there were no time there would be no decay or death. You think of an empty future – you feel robbed of the times you would have shared with your child as he grew up, with your partner when you retired. As a parent you assumed that it would have been you who did the leaving, as partner that it was you who was going to 'go' first. At a parting it is the one left behind who feels the loss most keenly. You are dominated by the idea of a life span – an arbitrary allotment of time.

But time also allows us to come to terms with change. Make time your ally. Life is now. Each life has its own length. It is a whole life. A life span is just an idea in your head. By living less than is expected he or she may also have missed much of the pain and suffering of life. Try to live in the present at all times. You may be walking in a beautiful park or by the river but often your mind is elsewhere, worrying about a hundred and one things, blaming others, feeling sorry for yourself, going over the loss again and again, resentful, envying, hating, fuming, exploding. You are walking – just walk. Look at the trees, the river, the clouds, the green moss as you pass slowly by. Breathe the fresh, cool air. Notice the gentle movement of the solidly rooted trees, the stillness of the earth they stand in. Notice each foot as it touches the ground. You share many molecules with the earth and the plants around you. You are co-existent. When you die you do not cease to be a part of this existence – you are transformed into dust, earth, water, air. New forms of life can spring from these elements. Without this constant interchange between coming together and dissolution, life could not exist. However independent we feel, however separate, cut off or isolated, we are a part of a habitat in which all life forms are dependent upon each other and ultimately upon the sun. The plants trap the sunlight which provides the energy which we need to survive. All our sophisticated methods of energy extraction are lost without that simple equation in which a photon transforms itself into a molecule of chlorophyll. Without it there would be no life, no culture, no civilization. We are part of a cycle of time which stretches back through the generations via our parents and grandparents and beyond to the beginnings of life.

The present moment contains the whole past, the seeds of whole future. Stay with that moment and you will be at the pivotal point. This is where you can find the balance and equilibrium that your bereavement has so cruelly disrupted. Let go of past pain, ease away from your fears and fantasies about the future. Release yourself from the dark dungeons and your vain hopes. As you breathe the living air of the present you are poised between the ebbing away of the past, and the rising wave of the future that will surely break – but has not yet broken – on the shores of life.

CHAPTER 11
MOODS AND THE FAMILY

'Before anything can be embarked upon in married life, there must necessarily be either absolute antagonism between husband and wife, or loving agreement. When relations are uncertain, neither one thing nor the other, no move can be made.' (Tolstoy)

Moods are infectious. If someone in a family is 'moody', it has a big effect on the way the rest of the group feels. Some families are dominated by a mother's bad tempers or a father's gloom. A miserable baby may make everyone in the family tense and exhausted. A whole family may go up and down on the rollercoaster of adolescent mood swings. The aim of this chapter is to discuss how this mysterious process of mood transmission occurs, and to offer some suggestions for dealing with bad moods within families.

dealing with bad moods within families

When we are in a bad mood other people can unwittingly be very useful to us. We dump our moods on them, rather as radioactive waste is conveniently taken out to sea and disgorged. But there is often a price to pay – the process works for a while, but it will eventually contaminate the relationship and has long-term consequences which have bad effects on our emotional environment. Three damaging

but common patterns of emotional waste disposal within families are :
- mood offloading
- blaming
- bad moods as a means of maintaining contact.

Mood Offloading

Some people are very adept at passing their bad mood on, as in a game of pass-the-parcel, so that when the music stops they are no longer holding it. The husband, who lies in bed last thing at night and says to his wife, 'I'm really worried about that gas bill' or 'Do you think we should do something about David's school report ?', and then promptly drops off to sleep leaving her to wrestle with the problem for half the night, is well versed in the art of mood offloading. Pressing home an attack when someone is themselves feeling vulnerable is another classic tactic. If you are feeling hurt or annoyed by something your partner has done, you may find yourself quite unconsciously waiting until they are slightly 'down', or have a cold or have had a setback, and then raising the issue that bothers you. More often than not you will find that as their misery increases you feel better. This marital game of mood see-saw is very common.

Blaming

Perhaps the most frequent way in which we use our family members or partners as an antidote to our bad mood is to blame them for it. After all, we think to ourselves, there must be some reason why I feel so angry or het up or miserable. Spouses and parents provide a readily available and plausible excuse for our unhappiness. She is fed up because he never helps out with the children, or brings his friends home for late night drinking sessions, or never seems to feel like sex, or always seems to want sex when she's not in the mood, or had that fling last year, or will leave his dirty clothes all over the floor and expect her to pick them up, or inflicts his demanding and difficult children from a previous marriage on her when all she wants is to be alone with him... He blames his bad temper on her lousy cooking, or her untidiness, or because she's always running to her mother, or because she can't stop mentioning that old boyfriend of hers, or because she never takes the initiative in sex, or expects him to put shelves up when he's just worked three twelve-hour shifts in a row...

EXAMPLE: A MELANCHOLY MARRIAGE

Phil and Clare met at a dance – she was 15, he 17. Six months later they were married, a merciful escape for Clare from her abusive father, and for Phil a chance to establish himself as a person rather than just being one of the six 'boys' in his large family. Phil worked as a postman, while Clare brought up their four children and supplemented the family income by babyminding and fostering. As the children began to need her less she started going to night classes. That led to correspondence classes and eventually she gained a place as a mature student at university. Phil found it hard to keep up with her intellectually, and she seemed to spend more and more time with her girlfriends and their teenage children who were also studying. He felt increasingly irrelevant in the family – 'Just someone who is there', as he put it. Clare felt correspondingly frustrated by his quietness, depression and lack of sexual interest in her. She put on weight, secretly blaming Phil for her self-neglect, he meanwhile blamed her for his depression. Then through work he met a young woman with whom he had a brief affair, which helped him to feel much more self-confident. He dealt with any guilt by blaming Clare – 'If only she had paid more attention to me it would never have happened'. Eventually he confessed and, after much mutual recrimination, they decided to stay together. Clare agreed that she had neglected Phil, while he saw how he had felt very angry with Clare but had expressed it indirectly by being unfaithful rather than confronting her.

A similar pattern is often to be found between parents and children, especially adolescents. Teenagers blame their parents for their feelings of frustration and depression. From the teenage perspective, parents can be boring, or stingy, or restrictive, or uninterested; they treat teenagers like children, or neglect them, or tell them what to do, or never bother to find out about them, or disapprove of them, or are unloving and uncaring. Likewise parents blame their children for using their home like a hotel, never going out or always going out, lying in bed all day, never lifting a finger and, generally, for the sleepless nights of worry and disappointment they cause.

EXAMPLE: DUMPED

Three years married, Petra and Mike were very happy together. He was divorced, with two sons in their early teens who visited once a month and for part of the school holidays. Petra had a busy secretarial job, while Mike was unemployed and looked after the house, which belonged to her. All went well until Mike's former wife announced that she was emigrating to the USA and that Mike and Petra could jolly well look after the boys. Petra, who had never found her stepmotherly role easy and who felt very jealous of Mike's relationship with his sons, suppressed her doubts for Mike's sake and welcomed the boys into her house. Although things were all right with the younger son, with Alex, the older boy, there were difficulties from the start. He was silent and sullen and refused to help with the household chores. He sat around all evening in their small house watching TV, so that Petra and Mike had little privacy. Petra became increasingly exasperated, furious with Mike for allowing things to develop in this way, and angry with Alex for his dumb insolence and refusal to respect or recognize her rights. When Mike remonstrated with her she felt even more isolated and betrayed. When rather half-heartedly tackled by Mike, Alex complained that Petra disliked him, and he didn't see why he should be civil or helpful to someone who clearly did not want him there. Eventually Petra decided to speak to Alex on her own. Initially he refused to talk, but when she let him know how hurt she felt by his intrusive silence and how she needed time alone with Mike, he started to cry and revealed how desperately he was missing his mother and how angry he felt about being dumped, as he saw it, on his father and stepmother without being first asked what he wanted to do.

There is often more than a grain of truth in blame and accusation. They raise issues that need to be tackled, changes that need to be made. But blaming someone, either in your mind or openly, does not usually lead to change. More often than not it provokes retaliation, a counter-attack which then justifies your continuing to see the other person as the cause of all your troubles. The object of your blame provides a reason for feeling bad, a target towards which all your horrible feelings can be directed, and if you can get them to start being beastly to you so much the better – that proves it's all their fault!

Bad Moods as a Means of Making Contact

A third aspect of how other people play a part in bad moods is illustrated by the teenager who warned her brothers and sisters 'Watch out, Mum's on the warpath; she's pacing round the house trying to find someone to have a row with'. Bad moods cut us off from people. We feel lonely and unlovable. We hate everyone and everything – and yet we long for closeness and acceptance. If, through our bad mood, we can provoke someone into having a row with us, then at least we have made some sort of contact. Like an Elizabethan battleship, we have thrown out a grappling iron which locks us together with a combatant and so have overcome our isolation.

Quarrelling-for-contact is frequently seen when couples have difficulty in communicating. As they slowly drift apart one of them provokes a furious row which forces them to focus on one another, even if that focus is one of

Quarrelling-for-contract

naked rage and hatred. At last they are showing their true feelings. Often the row is followed by an emotional breakthrough in which they begin to realize how much they need each other, and this may lead to a passionate reconciliation. Similarly, but in a less intense way, adolescents, caught between childhood and adulthood, need, alongside their relentless search for independence, to return frequently for nurturance from a secure home base. Sometimes the only way they can get through to their bewildered parents is to provoke rows and anxiety, and these too may end in tears and cuddles which would be hard for the teenager to ask for directly.

But why do we go to such lengths to embroil our family members in our moods and often in such unproductive or even destructive ways? The answer lies in the earliest bond between parent and child, where, as we suggested in Chapter 2, moods can be understood in the context of a relationship. Infants are filled with a host of sensations which they are encountering for the first time. Some are 'good' – warmth, satiation, being held and rocked. Others are 'bad' – hunger, pain, coldness, fear. The infant is also filled with the emotions evoked by these experiences – pleasure and excitement, frustration and rage. The child puts or 'projects' these feelings, especially the 'bad' ones, into the mother who is usually unperturbed by them, gradually soothing away or 'detoxifying' them.

EXAMPLE: WHY NAPPY-CHANGING MATTERS

Take a baby who wakes up in his cot, hungry, cold and wet. He (or she) starts to cry, insistently at first, demanding attention, then perhaps with rage when there is no immediate response, then with a note of fear in his voice as the possibility that he may not be responded to at all creeps into his consciousness. The mother (or father) appears at last – perhaps she has been asleep, or attending to another child. Immediately she goes into action. As she comes into the room she starts to talk to him, her soothing words at first drowned by his cries. She picks him up, holds him, wipes away his tears. He is screaming all the while. She feels the tension rise in her, but, unlike the baby she can hold it, tolerate the discomfort, knowing that all will be well in a few minutes. She lies him down to change his nappy, while he continues to scream and protest, kicking and flailing wildly. She holds him with just the right amount of firmness – enough to contain his protest and to enable her to do what is necessary, not so much that he is hurt or constricted. Finally he is clean and dry and ready to feed – she holds him to the breast or offers the bottle. Bliss! All is peaceful save for the sounds of contented sucking. He pauses for a moment and they gaze at each other, filled with mutual trust and love. All this is the most natural thing possible – it happens thousands of times a day all over the world.

But what has happened? The parent has contained the baby's fear and anguish and pain, secure in the knowledge that these feelings will be short-lived, soon to be replaced with pleasure and contentment. As we grow up so this process of containment goes on internally – we manage to cope with our own feelings of anxiety or rage or despair because we have built up a reservoir of experience from childhood which reassures us that all will be well, that bad feelings can be lived through, that as time passes, feelings change too – 'This too will pass'. But we cannot always do this for ourselves. We need our spouses and partners and parents as containers for bad feelings – and it is this that underlies the infectiousness of moods we have described. But, unlike contact between parents and infants, this process of mood projection goes in two directions. It may well be that just as you are trying to get your partner to take on your mood, she wants you to do the same for her. From being partners you suddenly become rivals, each vying for the other's attention. Why the hell should you listen to her woes when yours are so unbearably pressing? And of course she feels just the same. The stage is set for an all-too-familiar escalating row, in which each competes for the attention of the other.

Suggestions for Mood Containment in Relationships

This way of looking at family mood problems raises three questions-

- How can you deal with your bad moods without foisting them on others ?
- Can the problems in the relationship which have triggered the bad mood be tackled more productively ?
- As the recipient of the 'projected' moods, can you find ways of responding to them so that the sufferer is not rejected, but at the same time you are not overwhelmed with feelings which do not 'belong' to you ?

Avoiding Blaming

If you are feeling bad, your first task, rather than blaming someone else, is to deal with and contain your mood, along the lines suggested in the previous chapters. If your house is on fire it won't help if you chase after the arsonist – you need to get the blaze under control. You start worrying about who set it alight later. Remember that your 'bad' moods are part of you and that they are telling you something that needs to be heard, and then responded to. If you simply blame and attack others you lose touch with your feelings and may feel empty and confused. Take responsibility for your moods – welcome them back as you would a prodigal son. Your resentment, loneliness, sense of betrayal, are yours, no one else's – however much they have been provoked by another's behaviour. Your feelings are valid; no one can deny them or take them away from you. Only you know exactly how you feel. The more you get in touch with your own feelings – through mood brooding and inner dialogue – the less you will need to project your feelings onto others. You will now be in a much stronger position to confront people with your feelings, and let them know how they are affecting you.

If you feel angry with your husband, tell him so. Rather than 'It's all your fault I'm so ratty with the children and miserable all the time – you're never home, and even when you are, all you want to do is read the paper', try 'I feel angry and lonely a lot of the time. Perhaps you could do something to help change that?' In this way you will become active rather than passive. You will begin to take charge of your life. You will break the deadlock in which you blame your partner for everything that is wrong and he does the same to you. Each of you will start to acknowledge the other's feelings, and you will feel free to move closer towards one another or to

become active rather than passive

get further apart if that is want you really want. Your 'bad' feelings will now be working for you rather than against you, helping you to make positive moves in your life which will reduce your discontent.

EXAMPLE: TENDERNESS IN A MELANCHOLY MARRIAGE

When Phil and Clare, whom we described earlier, finally started to talk, she told him for the first time about her sexual abuse from her father. Phil was thunderstruck. He had always seen his wife as strong and competent, and far more intelligent than himself. Although he was hurt that she had not spoken about this before, when he saw her weeping inconsolably his heart was touched, and he felt a wave of tenderness and protectiveness come over him, which made him aware of his own strength and competence which he had projected into her, and of her vulnerability of which he had known so little.

Avoiding Being Blamed

If you are on the receiving end of attack and blame there is also much that can be done. It is all too easy either to agree to the attacks that are made upon you, especially if you have a tendency to self-blame and guilt, or to retaliate with your own grievances. The parent of the furious teenager who is accused of having neglected him or her as a child, dumping him with babyminders or, as in divorce, walking out, is faced with the seemingly impossible task of responding either by dismissing the protest – 'Nonsense, she was a very good babyminder and anyway I always made a fuss of you at weekends' – or guiltily rolling over – 'Yes I was a terrible parent, it's no wonder you are making such a mess of your life now, it's all down to me.'

EXAMPLE: GUILT, SCHMILT

A classic example of inappropriate parental guilt occurred with Esther, a loving but desperately overinvolved mother who took her children's every success and failure as her own. When her 30-year-old son rang to say that he would be late for his regular visit because his car had broken down, she immediately started to apologize as though it was all her fault.

As parents and children we need to be able to stand our ground, refusing to be brainwashed by the accusations, while at the same time taking them seriously, and deciding whether part of the criticism is true. Our accuser's feelings need to be acknowledged and respected without being kowtowed to or dismissed: 'Sometimes it was really difficult, but a lot of the time we did quite well'.

A basic principle of mood management in relationships is that you can, in the end, never change anyone but yourself. You may long for your partner to drink less, or to be more tidy, or for your teenager to study for his or her exams or to be less rude, and the temptation to try to deal with your own worry and exasperation by trying to get them to change is enormous. Here too you may need to confront them not with demands or nagging, but with your feelings: 'I'm really worried that you will fail your exams if you don't do some more work'; 'It upsets me a lot when you come home drunk, and I worry about what may happen to your health if you go on drinking like this'. Your partner may try to persuade you that you are just nagging him again, that it is 'your problem', not his. You must stand firm. You are just telling him as clearly as you know how about your feelings.

> *you can, in the end, never change anyone but yourself*

EXAMPLE: ANXIOUS ATTACHMENT

Rob and Jemima had been married for five years. Both had been married before. Rob's two children visited every other weekend, while Jemima's lived with them. They had a little girl of their own. It was a complicated setup that on the whole worked well. But whenever Rob had to go away on business trips Jemima felt terrible. In the days leading up to his departure she would become tense and irritable. While he was away she felt furious and abandoned, and imagined all the fascinating women he was meeting. On his return she was cold and rejecting. Rob found this incomprehensible and they had many rows about it. He felt she was manipulating him, and trying to get him to stay at home. She felt he did not care about her. Whenever she tried to talk to him about it he got angry – 'You don't understand. It's not that I want to go away from you, its just my job, I have to go. Why don't you try to be more grown up about these things?' Then one day, after yet another row, Jemima tried to explain yet again: 'It's not that I want to stop you going, but I want you to know how I feel'. There was a silence. Suddenly Rob saw a picture of Jemima feeling lonely and abandoned and jealous. He allowed the image of her unhappiness to come into his mind, rather than blotting her feelings out so as to make his own guilt and anxiety about separation more bearable. They began to talk. He told her how numb he felt when he was away, and they saw how Jemima was 'carrying' the pain of separation for both of them. Memories of past separations came back to them – their previous broken marriages, her sadness when her father was away fighting in the war, and his when his mother was ill in hospital for long periods. The rows stopped. Trips away became less problematic, and when Jemima started going away herself, Rob was able to tell her how difficult he found it. They agreed that leaving was much easier than being left.

Making Time

Another important principle is that difficulties are rarely solved in the heat of a row. Timing is all. Make a habit of finding time to talk about problems and emotional conflict in as calm an atmosphere as possible. As you talk, acknowledge to yourself the validity of the other person's feelings. Breathe deeply to help yourself remain calm, centred on your feelings and respectful of the other person's, however much they may try to deflect you from your purpose or seem to ignore you.

Set aside time for mood-brooding both on your own feelings and those of the other person. Picture yourself as a mother embracing and calming your feelings of hate and rejection. Bathe your wounds, cool your fury. When these intense feelings have subsided in your mind imagine your 'feeling-baby' can speak. In your inner dialogue listen carefully to what your baby is saying: 'I feel hurt. I long to feel close. I feel uncared for. I want to be held. I want warmth…'. When you talk with your partner or family member this will enable you to hold on to your feelings and not be diverted into nagging or blaming. If you are tender with yourself you will be open to others' tenderness, and less likely to reject efforts at reconciliation.

If your partner is hurt by something you have done, 'sit' on this issue. Picture them in their unhappiness, the rejection they felt when you betrayed them, or ignored their feelings. Enter their feelings in your mind, feel them yourself, as you breathe deeply with empathy and compassion. Do not be plagued by guilt and remorse, simply identify with your partner or child or parent in the safety of your visualization. Now in your inner dialogue find words to express your feelings towards them. They may be words of compassion and regret, a wish to make amends. Or you may simply say 'Yes I acknowledge how hurt and miserable you feel, I can see your pain, but I had to do what I did. I want you to forgive me, but if you cannot, I will understand that too'. If you can do this in your imagination you will find it easier to do in real life.

The 'Ten Commandments' of Family Life

Psychotherapists are sometimes accused of worshipping 'relationships' as though they were the only thing that really matters, at the expense of all the other important aspects of life – work, politics, the environment, friendship, religion, the arts, hobbies, sport. It is clearly mistaken to believe that the only route to happiness is through a perfectly harmonious sexual partnership. But much of the suffering and loss which leads to 'bad' moods arises out of relationships, or the lack of them. There is so much more to life than 'relationships', and yet it is often only within the security of close relationships (this can mean close friendships rather than sexual partnerships), that we feel free to explore the variety of life and to withstand its inevitable setbacks and disappointments – 'the thousand natural shocks that flesh is heir to'.

Family relationships have a life of their own, greater than the sum of the individual members. For relationships to succeed they have to be taken seriously but that involves being able to laugh at them as well. We need to think what is best not just for me or even you, but for us. We conclude this chapter therefore with the 'Ten Commandments' of relationships, which, if respected, can significantly alter the mood and atmosphere within a family.

1 Put your intimate family relationships at the centre of your being. If they are central and secure you will be able to turn outwards to the world with security and love.

2 Be loyal to your family – they are the only family you have got. Think about their good points, be proud of what they have given you.

3 If you are unhappy about your family or your relationships do not just moan about it. Talking to a neutral person often helps, but in the end you have to tackle the problem where it belongs. Have the courage and self-belief to think that your feelings are valid; trust your family to listen to what you need to say.

4 Make time to communicate with your family, to share your feelings and to deal with difficulties and problems which arise.

5 Respect the cycle of the generations. You are a link in a chain stretching backwards towards the past, forwards to the future. Think with gratitude of the care and love and hope which your parents brought to you as a baby, however much you also feel let down by them. Without them you would not exist. Think how your present actions will affect future generations, will have an impact down the years.

6 Do not deny, discount or overrule another person's feelings. In doing so you are killing the emotional life of your relationship.

7 Recognize the force of sexual jealousy within a partnership. Be mindful of the impact of your actions on your partner even if he or she does not 'know' what you are doing. There is perhaps nothing more undermining to a person than to feel sexually rejected.

8 Be open with your partner and family about your feelings. Secrecy about feelings is almost always destructive. Have the courage to talk about your feelings, however negative or hurtful they may seem. But be tactful and do not 'throw in the kitchen sink' during a row. Avoid exaggeration and generalization; never say 'You never...', or 'You always...'.

9 Be aware of the power of envy. Do not drag third parties into your relationships. If you are not getting on with your partner, try not to involve the children in your bitterness. Leave mothers-in-law and former partners out of it and concentrate on what is happening now.

10 Do not waste time comparing your relationship with other people's. Your family is the one you have got – make the most of it, make it better if you can. Value yourself and your own ability to give and receive love.

CHAPTER 12
GOOD MOODS –
AND OTHER QUESTIONS

'Everything that happens to you is your teacher. The secret is to learn to sit at the feet of your own life and be taught by it.' (Gandhi)

A book has to believe in itself if it is to get written. But that self-belief often closes off a number of important questions, which, if attended to, would interrupt the flow and undermine the coherence of the story as it unfolds. In this last chapter we shall pick up a number of doubts and loose ends which may have arisen, presenting them in the form of our responses to imagined questions from an interested but sceptical reader.

'What about Good Moods? You Haven't Said Much About What They Are Like or How They Can Be Achieved'

We have concentrated mainly on 'bad' moods because if 'bad' moods can be unblocked, good feelings often follow naturally. We have described the spectrum of 'bad' moods; similarly there are many different patterns and hues of 'good' moods.

Here are some examples of the variety of good moods :

- Neutral states of peace and equilibrium.
- Cheerful moods in which the world looks sunny and everything you do feels amusing and fun.
- Creative states in which your powers of expression and understanding and achievement are activated and when you feel that no obstacle is insuperable, no goal unrealizable.
- Feelings of love and compassion towards your fellow beings.
- Feelings of ecstasy and excitement that often arise when you are in love or have just had a baby.

- Feelings of pure joy that seem to alight on you for no obvious reason, like a beautiful butterfly on a perfect summer's day, and to disappear again in an equally inexplicable way.

The principles of removing emotional blocks, striving for balance and equilibrium, and living in the moment will, as they help to overcome 'bad' moods, contribute to the achievement of these positive mood states.

Just as we see in 'bad' moods the germ of something positive, so 'good' moods can have their negative side. Some people are frightened or overwhelmed by good feelings when they arise. For others, moments of happiness – which are essentially transitory – carry with them the unbearable threat of loss. They shy away from joy for this reason. We cry for joy perhaps in recognition of this mixture of sadness that accompanies happiness, just as the 'pure' states of grief we described earlier in the book can have a wholeness or even beauty about them.

The proximity of happiness can be threatening as it unblocks not only the prospect of joy but also the channels of doubt and misery that have been sealed as a protection against pain.

EXAMPLE: FEAR OF HAPPINESS

Joanne, now in her thirties, had all but given up the prospect of marriage and had settled for a comfortable solitary existence as a solicitor. She enjoyed her solitude and her animals and garden. She had had several relationships in her twenties with men who in one way or another had let her down – she always felt second best. Her childhood had not been easy: her mother had been a drinker and her father a spendthrift who was often away from home, leaving Joanne and her brother to 'look after' their frequently incapacitated mother. Then Joanne met a man whom she liked and who seemed fond of her. At first she assumed it would be another of her short-lived 'sensible' affairs, but she found that she was really fond of him and, what was worse, he of her! When he asked her to marry him she was thrown into confusion. All her self-doubt, and fear that things would inevitably go wrong, and incredulity that anyone could really want her, came to the surface. She felt like a fourteen-year-old in love for the first time. Happiness seemed to be only just visible through a mass of pain and failure which she had done her best to forget. By forcing herself to 'contain' these anxieties she accepted his (rather old-fashioned) proposal, but still found it hard to believe that she could have the right to love and be loved.

Another common experience is the mixture of happiness and disappointment that often goes with some long-anticipated achievement: an exam passed, a job offered, or such supposedly wonderful events as the birth of a baby or getting married. Along with the pleasure and relief there may be flat feelings of 'So what?', or thoughts like 'Was that all there was to it?', or 'I have changed, but the world looks exactly the same'. The longed-for ecstasy just isn't there, or is very short-lived.

When we are in love we are in a blissful heightened state. At times we feel a sense of satisfaction and fulfilment, perhaps seeing him or her as our salvation, our hope, our solution, our heart's desire. As soon as we become fearful of change, we start to cling and this exposes us to the possibility of more suffering. Now we have so much to lose – the more love we want, the more prey we are to jealousy and possessiveness. Being in love can be liberating, as can 'being in grief' or 'being in despair'. At such intense moments we see things clearly, not, as we usually do, 'through a glass darkly' but as they really are – everything seems to radiate its essential nature and to pulsate with life and beauty.

Just as the dark clouds of bad moods will pass, so too these moments of epiphany or enlightenment are also transient. The sun dims and ordinary reality returns. Some people find this unbearable and constantly seek to recapture the 'in love' experience. As soon as one object of desire loses its charm it is replaced by another, and another. Within each 'falling' there is hope and expectation – 'At last I've found what I was really looking for' – a sense of homecoming, of relief, of immense hope, like a child with his pile of unopened Christmas presents. But when the wrapping paper is removed there is a moment of disappointment. Nothing can equal the soaring fancy of those expectations and dreams.

This book could be called the 'good equilibrium guide'. Good moods need to be accepted, enjoyed, valued – but not seen as an end in themselves. The exclusive pursuit of good moods is as ensnaring as the feelings of trappedness that can come with bad moods. By being in a state of equilibrium we can witness and accept our moods, allowing them to arise in us and die away without losing touch with reality or becoming unbalanced in the process. We need to contain and brood our good moods as much as our bad ones, using breathing to reassemble and integrate the scattered self of excitement as much as the shattered self of despair. In this state of equanimity we observe all our feelings with clarity and compassion. We know that all our feelings originate from within us, and are our own reactions to circumstances: 'The mind... in itself can make a Heav'n of Hell, a Hell of Heav'n.' (Milton)

'Will It Work For Me? I'm Sceptical About All This "Magical Transformation" Business'

Changing old habits and patterns is hard. The suggestions for change we have put forward, although simple, are not easy. For them to 'work' for you, you have to work for them. Practising breathing and awareness on a daily basis, and facing your difficult feelings, requires application and courage.

The results are rarely instantaneous. Internal change has its own rhythms: occasional sudden, blinding realizations; more often slow and gradual strengthening progress; doldrumy feelings when nothing much seems to be happening; resistance and despair, as well as a sense of liberation and breakthrough.

We use the word transformation because it captures that essential moment of surprise and disorientation when 'bad' turns into 'good' before our very eyes, rather as in the 'figure-ground' experiments of psychologists an old hag turns into a beautiful woman, and vice versa.

Transformation will 'work' to the extent that you can, through breathing and awareness, take control of thoughts and feelings as they arise. If you can contain your 'badness' it will change so as to become manageable or even helpful. But you will not become immediately free of all that is troubling you. On the contrary, you will be introduced to aspects of yourself that you may have long avoided. You may for the first time begin to get in touch with supressed envy or anger, and although this broadens and opens you, it can also be shocking and disconcerting.

EXAMPLE: THE BAD INTERNAL PARENT

Annie, a divorced teacher in her forties, had suffered from depression for many years. She was familiar with breathing and relaxation and had used them, together with psychotherapy, successfully to cope with her unhappiness and difficult relationships. When her daughter had her first baby she once more felt the onset of depression and using the Mood Transformation Method visualized a small-child part of her that was crying and helpless. To her astonishment, the next image she had was of a furious mother wanting to batter the crying child. She abruptly stopped the visualization, feeling alarmed and distressed. In her next brooding session she concentrated on this angry mother who felt so overwhelmed by her baby's misery. This brought back a memory from her own childhood in which she was suffering from measles but left to cry behind two sound-proof doors, while her mother drank riotously with men friends. She returned to the image of the angry mother and saw her transform into an unhappy only child, spoiled and indulged by two doting but neglectful parents who had left her in the charge of an endless succession of nannies. Once she had traced her own 'bad' internal parent to her grandparents in this way she was better able to understand her depression and how the arrival of a grand-daughter had triggered it.

Scepticism can be very important. Within it is the recognition that major change is not to be undertaken lightly. A new idea needs to be held at a distance and considered from all angles before it is incorporated into your life, disrupting many habitual patterns and methods of coping. To be sceptical in this way is to show respect for the new ideas. Resistance is often a precursor to change. We call this (after the friend who first noticed it) the 'Dizzy Principle': whenever someone says they will definitely never do something, that is precisely what some time later, they may well will find themselves doing. After all, if they were not, at some level, considering doing it, why would they bother to announce so emphatically their opposition to it ?

EXAMPLE: THE DIZZY PRINCIPLE

Dan was a bright but timid five-year-old. One week before he was due to start his first term at primary school he announced that he was definitely not going to that horrid school 'where I would have to learn a lot of things I know already and model plasticine with people I don't even know'. Two weeks later he made further announcement: 'I love my school and am going to stay there for ever'.

Transformation is not a matter of 'arrival', but of continuation: the journey is what matters, not the destination. A good gardener's work is never done – he is always weeding and clearing and planting and tending his stock. A left-wing friend was fond of quoting at meetings the slogan of the South American revolutionaries: 'La lutta continua' – 'The struggle continues'. When he married he was surprised to discover that it applied to personal as well as political life: however happy a relationship, it needs constant attention if it is to remain healthy and happy. A yachtsman can't just set his course and then retire below decks to sleep. He has to be constantly aware of possible obstacles, to monitor and adjust to changes in wind, tide, weather.

'Isn't All This Looking Into Your Feelings and Setting Aside Time For Yourself Just a Form of Self-Indulgence?'

One friend accused us of encouraging a 'Religion of the Self'! Should not we be forgetting about our selves and our selfish needs and devoting ourselves to the service of others? Aren't we far too wrapped up in ourselves already, without needing yet more self-analysis, self-love, obsession with physical and mental well-being, at the expense of the suffering that surrounds us?

It is certainly true that, as one of the early critics of psychoanalysis put it, analysis (including self-analysis) can be 'the disease of which it purports to be the cure'. Self-preoccupation can become an end in itself, the quest for self-understanding a form of greed that distracts from truly facing oneself. One can become a therapy junkie. But the self which we have been encouraging you to get in touch with and nurture is not the narrow, 'selfish', self-serving, acquisitive self – although that part does need to be recognized and acknowledged – but a wider ecological whole, a true self that comprises all the 'good' and 'bad' parts that go to make up a complete human being. It is good if you are able to rise above the greedy, selfish, deluded 'ego' and to lose yourself in the service of others. But before you can lose yourself you must first find yourself. If you are frozen inside, the first step is to help you thaw so that your feelings can flow – then you can attend to others. The aim is self-collectedness, self-awareness – not selfishness. If you are in touch with your hatred and anger and misperceptions it will deepen your compassion for others. By attending to your own feelings – good and bad – you are contacting your better self. Our approach is not a religion of the self, but does involve emotional and spiritual changes which might be called religious, through becoming aware of a wider self which encompasses the highest as well as the most basic parts of your being.

'What is so Special About Breathing? Why Put Such Emphasis on an Ordinary Bodily Activity?'

In one sense there is nothing special about breathing. It is merely a convenient device for helping with concentration, and being able to concentrate one's mind is a great help in states of emotional distress. You could just as well think hard about your big toe, except that breathing is much easier to be aware of than big toes – we can focus our minds on our breath at will.

But, that said, there is something special about breathing, and it is remarkable that modern psychology and meditative techniques which have existed for thousands of years both recognize that controlling breathing is one of the most powerful methods for quietening anxiety and achieving peace of mind.

Our breathing is almost invariably affected by our moods. Breathing can be seen as a bridge that links the unconscious with the conscious mind, the emotions with the body, the inner world with the outside. It is both voluntary and involuntary – we can hold our breath or pant at will, and our breathing continues with its own rhythms and responses even when we are deeply unconscious. To repeat – if you can control your breathing you are well on the way to controlling your moods.

'You Talk About "Bad Moods" But Not About Mental Illness. Aren't You Encouraging People To Go It Alone When They Should Really Be Seeking Professional Help?'

This book is mainly about the reservoir of 'ordinary human misery' (as opposed to neurosis or psychosis) which afflicts so many people, but which does not mean that they are suffering from a mental illness. Bad moods can be perfectly normal. But bad moods that go on and on unremittingly, or are very severe, or in which our perception of the world becomes seriously distorted, can be signs of mental ill-health that requires professional help.

Society deals with misery and madness much in much the same way that individuals do – using denial and splitting as convenient mechanisms for dealing with unwanted or unacceptable aspects of life. Some people deny the existence of mental illness completely and advocate a pull-yourself-together approach. Others take up violent positions in opposing camps, either seeing drugs and psychiatric hospitals as dangerous and destructive and believing that everything can be solved with psychotherapy, or dismissing 'mere talk' as useless in the face of a disturbance of brain biochemistry. Just as individuals need to reconcile the splits within them between 'good' and 'bad', so a balanced approach to mental health will recognize the need for both psychotherapeutic treatment and physical methods, for professional assistance and self-help.

The more in touch with reality you are, the more likely you are to seek and receive help when you need it. Sometimes there is a need to save people from unnecessary medical treatment. There are still many people with emotional disturbance who are fobbed off with tranquillizers or antidepressants when what they really need is to be listened to, and to be helped to understand and value themselves. Even when outside assistance is being offered and accepted, self-help is still an essential part of recovery from mental illness or emotional disturbance. Often when people have recovered from a psychiatric breakdown and return to normal life they feel bereft of the support which has buoyed them up through their illness. They may feel they are just left to get on with it. By using the methods in this book you will find that there is always help available, even on a desert island – inside yourself!

'What Next?'

Most of this book is about you in relation to yourself rather other people. We have tried to meet you in that mysterious place, the world within, which each of us carries around inside us, and yet which extends without boundaries in all directions as far as the inner eye can see. This world is populated by thoughts and emotions, good and bad, by your observing self, by the powerful helping and guiding aspects of yourself. We have suggested dialogues and transformations that might take place amongst this gallery of characters and influences which inhabit you.

But, to paraphrase Andrew Marvell, 'the mind's a fine and pleasant place, but none I think do there embrace'. The internal work we have suggested will go a long way towards transforming your moods, but for this to be sustained you also need the help and support of other people who share, or at least understand, your feelings and philosophy.

Life – both mental and physical – is fragile. We can so easily be crushed, starved, fragmented – emotionally and physically. But the life force is strong too. We have many necessary defences which protect us. The body has the immune system. The mind has the transformative defence of grief and mourning, which is as basic to our emotional survival as wound-healing is to our physical integrity. A third and equally vital ring of defence is the network of people – parents, siblings, friends, partners, work-mates, and where necessary professional helpers – with whom, however hermit-like we may be, we are connected. Alone, we are vulnerable. Together we survive – physically, emotionally, spiritually.

We often feel imprisoned by our bad moods; far worse than any physical hardship for the prisoner is the severance from the protective human chain of family, friends, colleagues and fellow-beings that connects and protects and gives meaning to life. The political prisoner who knows that he is known about throughout the world is immediately strengthened in his resistance to oppression. The aim of this book has been to call an amnesty on bad moods – once you have acknowledged your feelings and can accept them, you will want to share them with others, to feel part of a community.

But where, you may ask, is this 'community'? Are we not more and more isolated and alienated as we live in our minute separate worlds, divided and apart from one another? How can we overcome the fear of rejection which stops us from making contact with the strangers we feel surrounded by? Here, once again, breathing and the transformative power of your inner visualization can help. As you sit and 'brood' on your fear and separateness, picture others torn like you between isolation and the longing to reach out and touch one another. Visualize the transformation of an inner world divided by hostility and suspicion into one where trust and shared feelings reign. You will sense the power of a group to protect its members from 'bad' feelings. As you change your inner world, so the way you perceive the outer world and the way it responds to you will change too. You become open to other people and to the world around you. 'Bad' and 'good' dissolve into one another. Hope and despair, destruction and creation, excitement and fear, joy and sadness cease to be opposites, becoming different aspects of an indivisible whole.

FURTHER READING

Faber, Adele and Mazlish, Elaine *How to Talk so Kids will Listen and Listen so Kids will Talk* and *Siblings Without Rivalry*. Practical help with actual child care, but principles apply to inner children as well.

Jeffers, Susan *Feel the Fear and do it Anyway*. How to overcome fears without running away from them.

Hay, Louise *You Can Heal your Life*. A good introduction to positive thinking, loving the inner self, and overcoming emotional barriers.

Holmes, Jeremy *Between Art and Science: Essays in Psychotherapy and Psychiatry, John Bowlby and Attachment Theory and Intimacy, Attachment, Autonomy: Clinical Implications of Attachment Theory*. More technical versions of some of the ideas in this book.

Levine, Stephen *A Gradual Awakening* and *Who Dies?* Many useful guided meditations (visualizations) on pain, illness and healing.

Nhat Hanh, Thich *The Miracle of Mindfulness* and *Being Peace*. Beautifully written accounts of how to achieve tranquillity while remaining engaged with the world by a Vietnamese Zen master now living in France.

Rycroft, Charles *Anxiety and Neurosis*. Simple readable account of some common psychological difficulties.

Siegel, Bernie *Love, Medicine and Miracles*. For anyone struggling with serious illness, this book by an American surgeon is inspirational.

Skynner, Robin and Cleese, John *Families and How to Survive Them*. Helpful for mood problems in families.

also available from

THE ORION PUBLISHING GROUP

☐ **Apples & Pears** £3.99
GLORIA THOMAS
0 75281 604 7

☐ **Arousing Aromas** £3.99
KAY COOPER
0 75281 546 6

☐ **Body Foods For Women** £6.99
JANE CLARKE
0 75280 922 9

☐ **Cranks Recipe Book** £5.99
CRANKS RESTAURANTS
1 85797 140 X

☐ **Eat Safely** £3.99
JANET WRIGHT
0 75281 544 X

☐ **Entertaining with Cranks** £6.99
CRANKS RESTAURANTS
0 75282 579 8

☐ **Health Spa At Home** £3.99
JOSEPHINE FAIRLEY
0 75281 545 8

☐ **Juice Up Your
Energy Levels** £3.99
LESLEY WATERS
0 75281 602 0

☐ **Kitchen Pharmacy** £7.99
ROSE ELLIOT &
CARLO DE PAOLI
0 75281 725 6

☐ **The New Cranks
Recipe Book** £6.99
NADINE ABENSUR
0 75281 677 2

☐ **Spring Clean
Your System** £3.99
JANE GARTON
0 75281 601 2

☐ **Vegetarian Slimming** £6.99
ROSE ELLIOT
0 75280 173 2

All Orion/Phoenix titles are available at your local bookshop or from the following address:

Littlehampton Book Services
Cash Sales Department L
14 Eldon Way, Lineside Industrial Estate
Littlehampton
West Sussex BN17 7HE

telephone 01903 721596, *facsimile* 01903 730914

Payment can either be made by credit card (Visa and Mastercard accepted) or by sending a cheque or postal order made payable to *Littlehampton Book Services*.

DO NOT SEND CASH OR CURRENCY.

Please add the following to cover postage and packing

UK and BFPO:
£1.50 for the first book, and 50P for each additional book to a maximum of £3.50

Overseas and Eire:
£2.50 for the first book plus £1.00 for the second book and 50p for each additional book ordered

- -

BLOCK CAPITALS PLEASE

name of cardholder ....

delivery address
(if different from cardholder)

address of cardholder ....

....

....

....

postcode ....

postcode ....

☐ I enclose my remittance for £.............................

☐ please debit my Mastercard/Visa (delete as appropriate)

card number ☐☐☐☐☐☐☐☐☐☐☐☐☐☐☐☐☐

expiry date ☐☐☐☐

signature ....

prices and availability are subject to change without notice